SPICES

Edible

Series Editor: Andrew F. Smith

EDIBLE is a revolutionary new series of books dedicated to food and drink that explores the rich history of cuisine. Each book reveals the global history and culture of one type of food or beverage.

Already published

Pancake Ken Albala

Pizza Carol Helstosky

Hamburger Andrew F. Smith

Hot Dog Bruce Kraig

Pie Janet Clarkson

Forthcoming

Bread William Rubel

Cake Nicola Humble

Caviar Nichola Fletcher

Dates Nawal Nasrallah

Cheese Andrew Dalby

Chocolate Sarah Moss

Cocktails Joseph M. Carlin

Coffee Jonathan Morris

Curry Colleen Taylor Sen

Fish and Chips Panikos Panayi

Ice Cream Laura Weiss

Lobster Elisabeth Townsend

Milk Hannah Velten

Pasta Kantha Shelke

Soup Janet Clarkson

Tea Helen Saberi

Tomato Deborah A. Duchon

Vodka Patricia Herlihy

Whiskey Kevin R. Rosar

Wine Marc Millon

Spices

A Global History

Fred Czarra

REAKTION BOOKS

Published by Reaktion Books Ltd
33 Great Sutton Street
London EC1V 0DX, UK
www.reaktionbooks.co.uk

First published 2009

Printed and bound in China by C&C Offset Printing Co., Ltd

British Library Cataloguing in Publication Data

Czarra, Fred R. (Fred Raymon), 1937–
Spices: a global history. – (Edible)
1. Spices – History 2. Spice trade – History
I. Title
641.3´383´09

ISBN-13: 978 1 86189 426 7

Contents

Introduction

Peppercorn, which has the ability to sweat your secrets out of you.
Peppercorn, where are you in my time of need?
The Mistress of Spices, Chitra Banerjee Divakaruni

We often marvel at the fascinating stories of spices and the exotic lands and peoples with which they are associated. At the same time, however, it is easy to overlook the historical context of these once highly prized commodities and the significance of the spice trade that developed around them. Spices are important in history for several reasons. First, on a large scale, they brought together diverse cultures of the western, southern and eastern worlds, encounters that could be positive and harmonious but were sometimes harmful and even disastrous. Second, the exchange of spices stimulated the first global age and the beginnings of economic globalization, wherein actions in one area of the world greatly affected people and events on another, far-off continent. Third, spices forever changed the eating habits of people who discovered new culinary experiences as a result of the trade, which in turn changed the way they prepared, ate and appreciated food.

Spices and their travels across the world have created new legends as well as enhancing the many tales and misconceptions that had preceded them. Spices stimulated new knowledge about the world, a knowledge that resulted in great advances in mapmaking, science, seamanship and basic cross-cultural awareness. They also created competition among nations, which improved the economic conditions of some countries and peoples but also caused great harm to others and to the cultures they encountered.

Spices had had a long history in South and East Asia long before Europeans arrived in these regions. During antiquity, the Old World had limited supplies of spices which were experienced by only a few cultures. Hearing of or sampling spices from places that the Europeans had never seen inspired numerous legends and tales – many of them of the tall variety – that fuelled misperceptions about these exotic lands and peoples. Such stories were sometimes tied to religion and the idea of paradise and where this land of perfection might be located. Spices conjured up the idea that exotic plants such as cinnamon were part of the scents of paradise. Once the Europeans encountered Asia, the realities of spices such as pepper coming directly home to a nation were more and more commonplace. The prices for these spices brought great riches. Additionally, when the word spread about these newly acquired products, competition became a strong motivator for nations to vie for both the prize and the profits.

In recent years, many excellent books have been written on spices. Titles such as *Nathaniel's Nutmeg*, *The Scents of Eden*, *Spice: The History of a Temptation*, *The Spice Route*, *Dangerous Tastes*, *The Taste of Conquest* and *Out of the East: Spices and the Medieval Imagination* have explored numerous avenues of spices and their lore. Most of these writings have offered a unique perspective on spices and, for the most part, have dealt with the spice trade in the ancient and early medieval world and from the sixteenth to the nineteenth centuries, when there was great competition between nations of Western Europe for these exotic and valuable products. These periods of history are the most engaging for story-telling, but more modern aspects of the spice story are also worth exploring.

The extensive focus of this general history of spices will range from antiquity to the present day. Its five chapters will explore the ancient world, the medieval world, the Age of Exploration, the Industrial Age and, finally, the age of globalization, extending through the twentieth century and beyond. *Spices* will be 'a global history' in the sense that different, at times contradictory, points of view about the spice saga will be presented, along with discourses on how diverse cultures have viewed and used spices in their lives. Finally, there will be an extensive bibliography of books on the history of spices, as well as on the spices themselves.

What are spices? A spice is usually defined as an aromatic part of a tropical plant, be it its root, bark, flower or seed. With the exception of vanilla, chilli pepper and allspice, nearly all spices are of Asian origin. Other spices such as frankincense and myrrh are only used for their aroma. Spices and herbs are sometimes viewed as the same thing but this is a fallacy. A herb is a plant that does not have a woody stem and dies at the end of each growing season. Most herbs derive their medicinal and seasoning qualities from their leaves.

To conclude, this section will take a first look at the five spices that are the focus of this book. This quintet, sometimes called the 'premier spices', have served as the motivators for the legends, the global searches and the economic competition that fuelled this trade.

The Premier Spices

There are many spices and mixtures of spices, but we will focus on the foremost five: cinnamon, cloves, black pepper, nutmeg and chilli pepper. Detailed coverage of their discovery, trade and uses will serve to illustrate the global movements of spices over time and the roles they played in world history. Other spices are mentioned in passing (cardamom, ginger and turmeric, for example), but this quintet provided the gold standard of the spice trade – not to mention heaps of gold and other riches for those sailors and merchants whose livelihoods depended on them.

Cinnamon (*Cinnamomum verum, C. zeylanicum*)

Cinnamon is derived from the Greek word for spice and the prefix 'Chinese'. The Greeks in turn got the word from the Phoenicians, who were most likely involved in sea trade with Eastern caravan routes controlled by the Arabs. Cinnamon and cassia are mentioned in the Old Testament and Sanskrit texts as well as in Greek medicinal works. Cinnamon is indigenous to the island nation of Sri Lanka (Ceylon), where it is grown on the coastal plains to the south of the capital city, Colombo. It comes from the bark of an evergreen tree of the laurel family. Tan and pale brown strips of dried bark are rolled into each other to form the cinnamon quills, or sticks. The seedlings grow in dense clumps of thumb-sized thickness. During the rainy season the shoots are cut off at the base and peeled. It is quite an art to cut the paper-thin strips of cinnamon from the bark and curl them into quills over 3 feet in length; these are then dried in the sun. The lighter the colour, the higher the quality. This spice has a sweet,

Laurus cinnamomum.

woodlike aroma with a taste that has elements of clove and citrus. Cinnamon is distinguished from cassia by an oil called eugenol. Cinnamon loses its flavour quickly, so it should be purchased in small amounts – though if the quills are kept in an airtight container, the flavour can last for a few years.

Cinnamon is very well matched with many desserts as well as cakes and breads. This spice goes well with apples, bananas and pears and is particularly suited to chocolate. Use cinnamon with bananas fried in butter with a little rum, or in apple pie. Cinnamon is used to flavour meats in India and in masalas, with other spices, and also in chutneys. In Morocco, the spice is used in lamb and chicken dishes. Cinnamon, especially from Sri Lanka, supplies the alcohol industry. Many liqueurs and bitters contain this spice. Cinnamon oil is made from the waste products of cassia and cinnamon.

In world history, the cinnamon trade out of Ceylon existed for centuries. Then, from the beginning of European expansion into the spice trade, control of the cinnamon market passed from the Portuguese to the Dutch and finally to the English. Because of an increased worldwide demand at the end of the eighteenth century, cinnamon was successfully replanted to the north in India as well as to the east in Java and in the Indian Ocean islands of the Seychelles, east of Zanzibar. Today Great Britain is a leading consumer of cinnamon, along with the United States and Spain.

Clove (*Syzygium aromaticum, Eugenia aromaticum*)

Cloves are native to the Moluccas, a group of volcanic islands that are now part of Indonesia. The clove tree is tall and ladders are needed to pick all of the clove flower buds, which are harvested when pink at their base and before they can open. The buds are dried in an open, sunny area on mats, losing most of their weight and turning a red to dark brown colour, at which point they are sorted. Clove buds appear in small clusters twice a year, from July to September and from November to January. All the work is done by

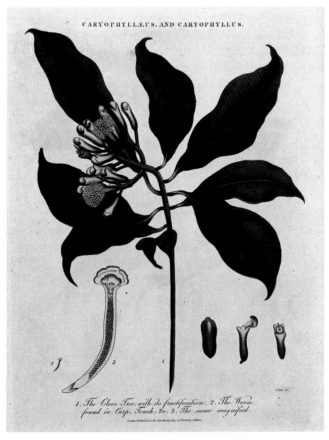

1. The Clove Tree, with its fructification. 2. The Worm found in Carp, Tench, &c. 3. The same magnified.

A clove branch. The clove flower is shown with its buds to the lower right and a parasitic worm on the left.

hand in a traditional manner. The scent of cloves has hints of camphor and pepper. They have a fruity taste that is also bitter and hot, and can make the mouth feel numb. In the seventeenth century a German botanist, Jiři Josef Kamel, identified the clove as a very powerful antiseptic useful for toothaches. As with cinnamon, the oil eugenol is essential to the taste that makes cloves unique. Good cloves should emit a small amount of oil and should break easily. They can be stored for a year in an airtight jar. The best cloves should have a red-brown stem with a lighter top, or crown.

Cloves can be used with both sweet and savoury foods. However, they have a very strong presence so should be used sparingly. Cloves are good with roasted meats such as pork or spiked on a ham with brown sugar (my favourite), with apples, beetroots, cabbage, carrots, onions, oranges or sweet potatoes. Cloves also mix well with other spices, such as cinnamon, chilli and nutmeg. They are used all over the world in mostly savoury dishes. In France a single clove is placed in an onion to flavour a stew or sauce, and in the Middle East and North Africa cloves are used in spice blends and for meat dishes and rice. In China and much of Asia they are used in spice blends, one of the best known of which is India's garam masala. In Indonesia, which uses most of the cloves it produces, the spice and tobacco are the main ingredients in the cigarettes known as kreteks (so named because of the crackling noise of the burning cloves). Today, cloves are grown on Madagascar, Zanzibar and the hilly island of Pemba (part of present-day Tanzania), north of Zanzibar.

Chilli Pepper
(*Capsicum annuum, C. frutescens, C. chinense et al.*)

The chilli is native to Central and South America and the Caribbean islands. There are so many variations of chillies, and they come in so many shapes and colours, that it is impossible to define them as a unique spice, as is the case with nutmeg. Most chillies are grown as annuals. Green chillies are picked three months after planting. Chillies that are eaten ripe are left on the vine longer. Normally chillies are dried in the sun, but they may also be dried artificially. They affect the taste buds in a variety of ways: as a fruity or flowery taste, or perhaps in a pungent, smoky, nutty sense, or even with a liquorice or tobacco taste. The degree of heat in a chilli can vary from mild to extreme. The heat of chillies is measured by the Scoville Heat Index, named after the pharmacist William Scoville, which measures the capsaicinoids in a pepper by looking at their heat-creating molecules. In 2007 Paul Bosland, a professor of horticulture and the director of the Chilli Pepper Institute at New Mexico State University in Las Cruces, established the hottest chilli on record. A chilli pepper called *Bhut Jolokia* (or *Naga Jolokia*), from the Assam region of north-eastern India, registered on the heat index at 1,001,000 Scovilles. By comparison, the New Mexico green chilli registers at 1,500 Scovilles and the jalapeño at 10,000.

Chilli peppers contain two valuable vitamins, A and C, and will keep in a cool place for a week or so. If stored in an airtight container, they may keep for an indefinite period of time. The Spanish were the first to bring chilli peppers to Europe, but it was most likely the Portuguese who helped spread them into South and East Asia, where they are used more than anywhere else in the world today. India is the largest producer and user of chillies; the Chinese include them in a number of sauces; while the Koreans make a sticky condiment, called *gochu-jang*, by mixing chillies with soya paste and rice flour. In Mexico the chilli is used as a vegetable, as a sauce and in salsas, pickles and stuffings. In the Caribbean the very hot Scotch bonnet is used in sauces and jerk seasoning. To the north in the United States, the tabasco chilli (from which the eponymous hot sauce gets its name) and the chipotle are used in many commercial sauces.

In Europe it is Spain, Portugal and Hungary where peppers are most integrated into the cuisine – and culture.

Nutmeg and Mace (*Myristica fragrans, M. argentea et al.*)

Nutmeg is native to the Banda Islands of Indonesia and grows on an evergreen tree that can reach as much as 65 feet (20 metres) in height. Nutmeg is round and shaped like a small peach or apricot. In harvesting, the outer flesh and the interior covering of lacy red mace are stripped off, leaving a hard black/brown shell. The shell is dried on trays for one and a half to two months until the internal kernel, the nutmeg, rattles in the shell. The nut is then taken out and either grated or kept whole. The red mace is removed, flattened and dried for a few hours until it takes on an orange-red hue. The nutmeg kernels can be kept fresh in airtight jars for very long periods of time. You can also buy nutmeg graters containing a storage area with lid where you keep the nut, ready for use. The nutmeg yields about ten times the volume of mace, making mace more costly and less used in some nations. Nutmeg/mace is also grown in Penang, Sri Lanka, Sumatra and the West Indies, where Grenada once produced one-third of the world crop. In 2004, however, Hurricane Ivan swept through this island nation and devastated the nutmeg industry, which is expected to take almost a decade to recover.

Nutmeg and mace are highly versatile spices that complement many foods and combine well with other spices. Nutmeg is used on vegetables such as cabbage and cauliflower and on fruit puddings, all of which are Dutch favourites. Italians, along with others, like to put ground nutmeg on spinach. Malaysians use half-ripe nutmeg, boiled and

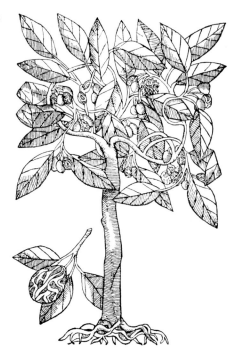

Nuez Moscada, from *Colloquies on the Simples and Drugs of India* by the Portuguese physician and naturalist Garcia de Orta, *c.* 1530s.

soaked in syrup, as a sweetmeat. The Arab world has long used both nutmeg and mace to spice up lamb and mutton dishes. Consuming too much nutmeg, especially in combination with alcohol, can cause the same reaction as a powerfully toxic drug. Today, because of this, nutmeg is banned in Oman and Saudi Arabia.

Pepper (*Piper nigrum et al.*)

The black pepper we know as *Piper nigrum* had its origins on the Malabar coast of south-western India. It was known for thousands of years across the world, making it to various points of

Fanciful view of a black pepper harvest on the Malabar Coast of India, from an early 15th-century French manuscript, the *Livre de Merveilles*. Harvesting black pepper is never this neat and clean. Pepper vines attach themselves to nearby trees and produce their green berries.

the compass by way of trading caravans and a seaborne network of small ships that visited ports from the Indian Ocean eastwards. Pepper grows on vines that are attached to trees. The leaves are a pointed v-shape with a long, dangling string of pendant berries parallel with the leaves. These immature berries are picked, very quickly fermented and then dried. During the drying process, the pepper becomes shrivelled and wrinkled and turns a dark brown or black colour. For white peppercorns, the berries are picked when yellow-red, and then soaked to get rid of the outer skin; once done, they are rinsed and sun-dried. Warm and woody on the tongue, black pepper has a sharp, biting taste sometimes with a lemon fragrance. White pepper is less aromatic because its oils are removed during soaking, but it is sharper to the taste.

This spice is also grown in Indonesia, Brazil, Vietnam and Malaysia. With its fruity aroma and clean bite, the Indian pepper of Malabar is still considered the best black pepper. Indonesian Lampong pepper has less oil, which makes it more pungent and less fruity. The best white pepper is considered to be Muntok from Indonesia. Pepper should be bought as peppercorns, since the spice retains its freshness longer in this form.

Pepper is neither sweet nor savoury but is used in numerous savoury dishes. Pepper can also be an ingredient in sweet foods such as breads and cakes, and it can be served with fruit. Simply put, it goes well with most foods, which is why it is so popular. It is also mixed with other spices to create the spice blends baharat and garam masala which are popular in Arabic and Indian dishes respectively.

I

Spices in the Ancient World

Be still! Oh north winds, and come, oh southern breezes,
and blow upon my garden, that the spice trees therein may
blossom and bear fruit!

The Song of Solomon

The ancient world was a hotbed of spice trading. It was a
thriving parallel universe of sorts that Western Europe knew
little about, stretching from China south to South East Asia
and west to India and Arabia. For more than 3,000 years
this world existed on its own and was connected with the
Mediterranean from the south-west to Arabia and Africa
and from the north-east by way of the Silk Road across
Central Asia. The spice trade was underpinned by a complex
system of sailing ships and overland caravans. The ships
were driven by the monsoon winds, which blew south in the
winter and north in late summer. These seasonal winds set
the timetable for trade and established a strong pattern for
the exchange of spices.

In the 500 years before the Common Era (CE) began, the
Greeks and Romans were at the height of their power, while
in Asia Confucius had developed his ethical system and the
Han Dynasty had become a dominating force in China. The

Saffron, the most expensive spice in the world, was used by the Persians as a flavouring and dye. Starting in the Near East, the spice was later grown in Europe. In the ancient and medieval world it was one of the few spices exported to China and India.

Greeks had established strong city-states and defeated the Persians. Philip of Macedonia and his son Alexander conquered the Greeks and Persians and extended their empire from the Mediterranean to the Himalayas. Rome became a major urban centre and was soon to expand its empire west into Spain, then into North Africa and Eastern Europe, and later north to Germany.

Cinnamon

During this era, the Greek historian Herodotus wrote of cinnamon which he had learned about from the Phoenicians. The Phoenicians had claimed that cinnamon sticks were brought to Arabia by large birds that carried them to their nests on mountain precipices. In order to get the cinnamon, Arabians cut up the bodies of large animals and placed them on the ground near the nests. When the birds picked up the food and returned to their nest, the weight of the meat broke the nest and the cinnamon fell down the mountain, where the Arabians ran to pick it up. The spice was then exported to other countries. Another variation of the tale has the cinnamon used by birds as nest-building material in trees, with the natives shooting arrows tipped with lead to break up the nests and bring the cinnamon down. These stories are perhaps a little far-fetched but, for those who traded these spices to people from far-off lands, such hyperbolic tales of hardship may have increased a product's value to the consumer and hence brought more profit to the trader and his supplier.

Cinnamon, in these times, was known to come from India and was later found on the island of Ceylon (present-day Sri Lanka), south of India. By the nineteenth century the cinnamon legend still persisted, as demonstrated by the Irish poet Thomas Moore:

> Those golden birds that in the spice time, drop
> About the gardens, drunk with that sweet food
> Whose scent hath lured them o'er the summer flood,
> And those that under Araby's soft sun
> Build their high nests of budding cinnamon.

Canela (cinnamon).

In the ancient world, cinnamon was the most sought-after spice. It was known in China as 'Kwei' as early as 2700 BCE and was introduced into Egypt around 1500 BCE. Throughout South and East Asia, China controlled the trade on cinnamon, even though it was not grown in that country. Ceylon emerged as a major source centuries later, when cinnamon was exposed to a wider world.

Other tales of cinnamon in the antiquity came from a Greek student of Aristotle, Theophrastus, who later became known as the 'father of botany'. He claimed that this spice

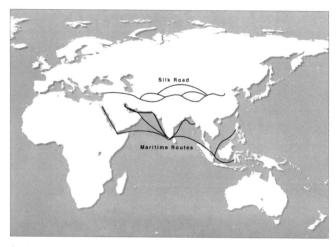

Ancient spice routes: land and sea routes between east and west in the ancient and medieval world. Notice how the sea routes take advantage of the Persian Gulf and the Red Sea to bring spices close to the Mediterranean, where European traders took them north.

came from Arabia, where it grew on bushes in ravines guarded by poisonous snakes. Those who got the cinnamon divided it into three piles and then chose two of the piles by drawing lots. What remained was left as an offering to the sun god, who would then protect them from the snakes on return visits. One Sicilian claimed that there was so much cinnamon in Arabia that it was used as fuel for cooking.

The ancient world had its legends of the 'Cinnamon Route', which began in northern Indochina and southern China and moved down through the Philippines. It then went into the East Indies to pick up more cinnamon and other spices and moved west across the long expanse of the southern Indian Ocean. Heading north-west, the route found land just off the north-west coast of Madagascar in an area known in Greco-Roman literature as Rhapta, near the present-day border between Tanzania and Mozambique.

The cinnamon was subsequently taken up the coast and dropped off at ports on the Red Sea.

Cassia

A spice closely related to cinnamon is cassia. It is native to Assam in northern India and Burma (known today as Myanmar) and on some Indonesian islands where it grew wild. Records on this spice go back about 6,000 years. Cassia is thicker and coarser than cinnamon, although the two are sometimes sold as the same product. The taste of cassia is less delicate than that of cinnamon and, because of this pungency the buds or dried unripe fruit of the cassia tree are used in pickles in the Far East. Cassia has its own, probably apocryphal, tales from the ancient world. According to Herodotus, the Arabs

> wrap their entire bodies and faces with skins and leather, except the eyes, and go out looking for cassia. It grows in a shallow lake, whose waters and borders are inhabited by a kind of winged animal, most like a bat. These creatures, squeaking loudly, defend themselves and their cassia with great courage. One must shield one's eyes from their attacks while gathering the cassia.

Clove

The clove had its origins in the Moluccas, or Spice Islands, of present-day Indonesia (they are called the Maluku Islands today). Its growth was originally confined to five of these volcanic isles, including Tidore and Ternate, both east of the

Clavos (clove).
'Clavos' also
means 'nails' or
'spikes' in Spanish.

northern spine of Sulawesi. The clove tree, an evergreen,
loves a tropical climate with rich soil. It does not prosper near
the sea, where there is too much moisture, nor in higher ele-
vations, where it is too cold. Sloping land with clean water
suits it best. One description, from the *Summary of Marvels* by
Ibrahim ibn Wasif-Shah, written around 1000 CE, reads:

> And somewhere near India is the island containing the
> Valley of Cloves. No merchants or sailors have ever been
> to the valley or have ever seen the kind of tree that pro-
> duces cloves: its fruit, they say, is sold by genies. The

sailors arrive at the island, place their items of merchandise on the shore, and return to their ship. Next morning, they find, beside each item, a quantity of cloves . . . The cloves are said to be pleasant to the taste when they are fresh. The islanders feed on them, and they never fall ill or grow old.

Spices in the Roman Empire

As the Roman Empire grew, the need for more spices increased as well. Of cloves, cinnamon, nutmeg and black pepper, the latter was the flavouring mainstay of the Romans (who did not use nutmeg in their dishes). The clove came late to Rome, in the second century BCE, and was mostly used in incense and perfume. There was also a 'Clove Route' that progressed from the East Indies, through South East Asia to the area near present-day Bangladesh and then down the east coast and up the west coast of India, from where it either went north to the top of the Persian Gulf at Basra or west to the Red Sea and its ports. Cinnamon was extremely expensive and was bought up by the perfume industry and favoured in wine and in some sweet and savoury dishes. One Roman emperor returned from Palestine with garlands of cinnamon, enclosed in polished gold, and Nero supposedly burned a year's supply of cinnamon and cassia at his wife's funeral rite. The Romans also used a perfume and salve called *malabathron* made from a form of cassia. Although available throughout the empire, nutmeg, as far as we know, did not appear in Roman dishes. One writer who researched Apicius' *Roman Cookery Book* found that 90 per cent of the 500 recipes in his book called for costly imported spices, especially black pepper. In 24 BCE, when Aelius Gallus was the Prefect of Egypt,

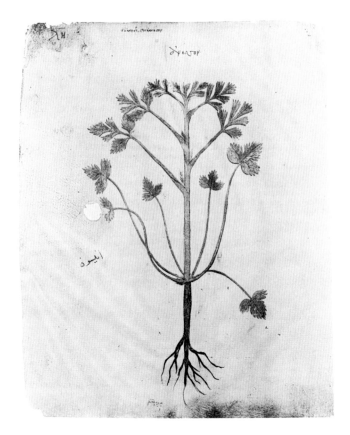

Anise is one of the oldest known spices and is related to caraway, cumin, dill and fennel. It is native to the Middle East.

the Emperor Augustus tried to break the Arab monopoly by using his Egyptian troops to take over those commercial routes from the East that were not controlled by Rome. It turns out that Gallus did not ask enough questions of local merchants about where the commercial routes were so he covered the coast with his army and missed out on the lucrative spice sites in the interior. Strabo points out in the

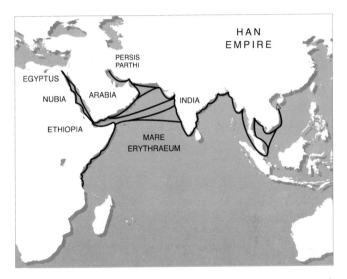

When the spice trade moved west, Mare Erythraeum, the ancient name of the Arabian Sea, bordered by India, Persia and Arabia, formed an active shipping area that transported spices north.

Geography that sickness, fatigue and hunger defeated the Roman soldiers more than any enemy. It was soon after this incident that emissaries from India, hearing of the fame of Augustus, came from India to Rome to meet with him and to set up trade networks.

Pepper, in at least two varieties, was the most widely used spice in the Roman world. Pliny the Elder described long pepper (*Piper longum*), grown in northern India, as a major source of Roman spice. Black pepper was not as popular as long pepper, which was much hotter to the taste. One Roman dish was chopped mushroom stems mixed with honey, garum (a sauce made of fermented fish) and pepper ground with lovage and then cooked in oil over low heat until the moisture had evaporated from the mushrooms; it was served with bread. Pepper was so important

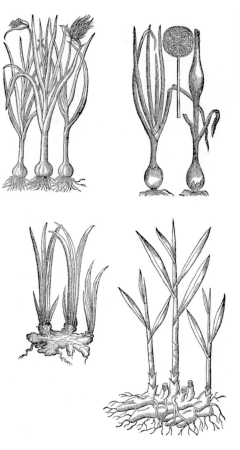

Ginger plant. Both ancient China and India used ginger. Rich in Vitamin C, it was eaten by early Chinese mariners to ward off scurvy.

that it had a custom duty attached. This tax was levied in Alexandria where the pepper came into Egypt from Arab traders. Keeping in mind how long the spices had to travel to reach Rome, across damp seas and dry land, it is no wonder that many of the spices that reached the centre of the Roman Empire may have been contaminated with bacteria and mould spores as well as dirt after much handling and storage.

Earlier, in the first century BCE, when the Romans were in Egypt, they discovered a new world of spices that the Egyptians had been using for centuries in various rituals and ceremonies, among them burials. Of special importance were frankincense, myrrh and cassia, all of which came from southern Arabia, where the air was scented with their aroma. Historically, the Egyptians had an exchange not only with Arabia but also with South and East Asia. At one point Egypt had built a canal connecting the Nile with the Red Sea to speed up the importation of spices from the Indian Ocean. Cinnamon can be traced to Egypt in *c.* 500 BCE. Recently, an archaeologist claimed to have smelled cinnamon when working on an ancient Egyptian mummy, but real evidence for very ancient traces of this spice are hard to come by.

On the Red Sea in the far south of Egypt's Eastern Desert is the site of Berenike. In the Roman period, this place was a trade emporium for spices coming up from the south. Five hundred miles south of Suez, Berenike was a major hub of trade with the Roman Empire. Emperor Augustus established a fleet of ships to bring black pepper and other exotic goods back to Rome. Recent excavations at Berenike have uncovered numerous peppercorns. Peppercorns of the same vintage – first century CE – have been found as far north as Germany, indicating that trade in spice had widened its geographical reach in Europe.

Cloves were praised early in the Sanskrit literature of India. They were called *katukaphalah*, 'the strong scented'. Pliny the Elder writes of them as only being imported for their aroma. In 335 CE Constantine the Great sent 45 kilograms of cloves to Pope Sylvester I, neatly packed in jars. Over time the clove came to be used in food and drink. In the ninth century, in the Gallen monastery in Switzerland, monks put this expensive spice on their fasting fish. In the

CUMIN SEED

Family: Umbelliferae لَعو'نون

كرنـ بسنان

Cumin. This spice is a native of the Nile Valley and was widely known in the ancient world. The Greeks used the word 'miser' to apply to someone who counted cumin seeds.

late 10th century an Arab traveller saw the burghers of Mainz seasoning their meals with clove. St Hildegard discussed it in her book about medical plants, *Liber subtilatum* of 1150. Even as far north as Norway and Sweden Queen

Fenugreek is a kind of pea plant. Its name is from the Latin for 'Greek hay'. It is used in *injera*, a sort of leavened pancake unique to Ethiopia.

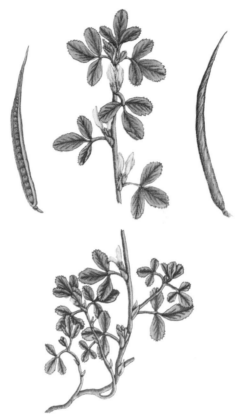

Blanche's estate listed three-quarters of a kilogram of cloves – a large amount for 1363.

Pepper and Other Spices in China

Far to the east, in China, records of the Han Dynasty from around the second century BCE indicate knowledge of a plant known as *Piper nigrum*, which was supposed to be from the west of China. It is most likely that the pepper had come from the opposite direction, east from India. Five centuries later, in the late Han Dynasty, pepper is clearly identified as having originated in India. Early records also indicate that pepper was also grown in household gardens in what is northern Vietnam today.

These were not the only sources of pepper in Asia. Historians say that black pepper was first cultivated in Java by Hindu colonists, who carried it there in around 100 BCE. Java may have been the main source for Chinese pepper, since it was more accessible than western India by sea. However, pepper in China was not easily available and was considered valuable and suitable for hoarding. It is a known fact that pepper was part of the diet of the Chinese people. They also used long pepper, which was hotter, in their dishes. Over time, pepper in Chinese dishes served as a substitute for *fagara*, which we know as Sichuan (formerly, Szechwan) pepper (*Zanthoxylum piperitum* et al.). The Chinese used pepper in medicine as a stimulant, tonic for digestion and relief from colic and flatulence.

Cinnamon first enters Chinese records as cassia cinnamon, grown in gardens around present-day Hanoi during the Han Dynasty. Cassia was also grown in southern China in Guangdong (Kwangtung), the geographic area that encircles modern Hong Kong. The name of the countryside city of Guilin (Kweilin), in north-east Guangdong, is translated as 'cassia forest'.

Cloves enter Asian history growing wild in the forests of New Guinea and on many of the Moluccas, where they are thought to have been domesticated. It does not appear that the natives of these clove islands had much desire to use them. However, the Chinese and Indians *were* interested and they initially stimulated and then conducted the

Pimienta (black pepper).

clove trade throughout Asia. Cloves appear in India in the literary classic *Ramayana* somewhere in the 400 years before 250 CE. Nan-Yueh seafarers from the modern Guangzhou (Kwangchow) area of southern China – long known in the West by the name Canton – brought cloves there from the Moluccas in the first millennium BCE. In the third century BCE, cloves are suggested as a breath freshener to be used by courtiers in the presence of the Han emperor. Their early name in China was 'chicken-tongue fragrance'.

Myristica fragrana. Nutmeg was native to the East Indies but has been successfully grown in the Caribbean on the island of Grenada.

There is a possibility that nutmeg was used in ancient China. During the Tang Dynasty (618–907 CE), this central seed of the fruit of an evergreen may have functioned as a medicine for diarrhoea and digestive problems. It is also possible that the Hindus of Java conducted a trade in nutmeg, as well as cloves, during this period, moving westwards from Indonesia to India. From this point the Arabs took the spices north-west to Europe. Nutmeg was cultivated much later in the Canton region (by the eleventh century). One of the mysteries surrounding nutmeg is whether it grew wild or not. This has been difficult to establish, one reason being that during the seventeenth century the Dutch went to other islands where it was grown and destroyed the nutmeg trees – in order to preserve their monopoly on the product.

Chillies, or Chilli Peppers

Many of the aforementioned spices that were used in the ancient world have had a lasting effect on food and medicine across the globe. But the chilli pepper, the most ancient and far-flung of spices, has had the most dramatic impact of all on comestibles and cultures worldwide. History – from ancient to recent – has shown this spice to have far more variations and types, and to have a wider range, from the Caribbean to China, than any other such aromatic seasoning.

There is evidence that chillies were eaten by Native Americans in what is now Mexico as early as 7000 BCE and cultivated a few centuries later. They were also indigenous to Central and South America and the Caribbean islands. Their debut on the world spice stage would not happen until the fifteenth century and the dawn of the Age of Exploration, but all their various types were growing wild and cultivated for food millennia earlier.

The ancient world has left its legends and uncovered many mysteries of spices. In the Middle Ages the West, under the banner of religion and in the form of the Crusaders, marched south-east and a new chapter on spices in world history was written.

2

Spices in the Medieval World

Robbed of your bark in masses large,
It's sent abroad by ship and barge;
And India's fragrance you bestow,
In summer climes and frigid snow.
Spices and How to Know Them, W. M. Gibbs

The early modern world and the world of spices were shaped by several significant events. The first was the decline of Rome's empire by 500 CE and the subsequent loss of the spice-trading networks that the Romans had established. Next was the birth of Muhammad in *c.* 570 CE. By the end of the first decade of the seventh century, Muhammad was preaching in Mecca, asking Arabs to throw away their old idols and demons and to follow one god, Allah. By the year 1000, Islam had spread north to southern Spain and east to the Malay Peninsula. In Europe, the continuous warring between different tribes and geographic areas in their quests for power was finally subsiding, leading to the establishment of more stable political regions. Near the beginning of the eleventh century, the Roman Catholic Church had grown in size and power and was asking rulers of these regions to band together to focus on recapturing the Holy Land, with its key city, Jerusalem, from

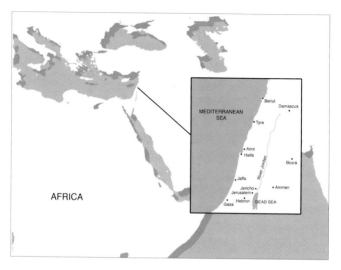

Spice trading areas during the Crusades. This area of the Mediterranean was vital to the shipment of spices west to Europe.

Islam. The Church had divided into an Eastern (Orthodox) and a Western (Roman) branch but, despite this split, and until 1302, the Crusades consumed both factions, greatly influencing as well the ebb and flow of spices. Finally, this period of history produced two renowned and prolific 'reporters', the near-contemporaries Marco Polo and Ibn Battuta, from the Christian and Muslim worlds respectively. Both travelled widely throughout the East and West, all the while describing new worlds and networks across Europe, Asia and Africa.

Muhammad was a spice trader who married a spice trader. This fact is indicative of the trading world that Islam had already established after the eighth century. With the growing strength of Islam came the rise of cities, first in Syria and then Baghdad, located on the Tigris, and north-west of Basra, which had been a major hub of the eastern spice-trading route for centuries.

In 711 Tariq ibn-Ziyad and his Muslim army had crossed the Mediterranean into southern Spain to establish a region that remained under Arab control until 1492. New Muslim–Arab cities grew up in this area, which was called Al Andulus, or Andalusia. By the 1100s, Cordoba was one of the great world cities, a Muslim centre of learning and a northern terminus of the Arab world. From Baghdad to Cordoba, these metropolises became not only producers of manufactured goods but also major consumers of Eastern spices. And throughout this part of the world there was continuous growth. Basra's population exploded from zero to 200,000 in three decades, its streets filled with Arabs, Persians, Indians and Malay-speakers from Indonesia. This was a place where information about China and the Spice Islands worked its way into legends and there was an over-all expansion of geographic awareness. In *The Book of One Thousand and One Nights*, Sinbad the Sailor recounted his journey to the Spice Islands:

> I went down to Basra with a group of merchants and companions, and we set sail in a ship upon the sea, and at first I was seasick because of the waves and the motion of the vessel, but soon I came to myself and we went about among the islands, buying and selling.

Sinbad was describing a route that had existed for over 3,000 years. From Basra, the Arabian Gulf was easy to sail since sailors never were out of sight of land as they moved east. The trade with the East was carried on by Arab, Iranian and Jewish merchants. These traders sailed on Arab ships that had gone as far as China but later concentrated on India and the East Indies. Over time it was found to be more con-venient to arrive at some halfway point such as Ceylon or

An Arab spice merchant weighing spices in a marketplace. Long before the Portuguese sailed to India, Arab merchants and middlemen facilitated the spice trade between East and West.

Malacca on the Malay Peninsula to receive goods from China. Certainly this was a more practical and cost-effective way of doing business.

While spices are the focus of this book, it should be noted that the great majority of ships in the Indian Ocean carried textiles, rice, hardwoods, iron ore, tin, horses and rope. To get a sense of the nature of international trade in the ninth century, consider this account by Ibn Khurradadhbih, a postal official in Baghdad, of a group of traders comprising Jewish merchants from the Frankish Empire (present-day France and western Germany):

> These merchants speak Arabic, Persian, Greek, Latin, Frankish, Spanish, and Slavic. They travel from West to East and from East to West, sometimes by land and sometimes by sea. From the West they bring eunuchs, female slaves, young boys, brocades, beaver, marten and other furs, and swords. They sail from the land of the Franks on the Western Sea [Mediterranean], and make for al-Frame [on the Isthmus of Suez]. There they transfer their merchandise to camels and go overland to the Red Sea port of Qulzum . . . From there they set sail and make for al-Jar and Jiddah. Then they sail to Sind, India, and China. On their return from China, they bring musk, aloeswood, camphor, cinnamon, and other products of the East. They return to Qulzum, then back to al-Farama, where they take ship once again on the [Mediterranean] Sea. Some sail to Constantinople, to sell their merchandise to the Greeks, others go to the capital of the king of the Franks to sell their goods.

These tradesmen also might have taken another, more eastern, route, heading south on the Euphrates to Baghdad, then down the Tigris to the Persian Gulf and on to India and points east. Either way, there is a historical issue about whether these long-distance travels were factual, especially before the tenth century CE, when knowledge and networks became more established. Trade also existed to the west into Arabia and East Africa, where the Ethiopian Christian kingdom of Aksum existed. This was the place where, according to biblical tradition, descendants of Solomon and the Queen of Sheba brought the Ark of the Covenant from Jerusalem. It was also here that gold and incense came out of Africa and moved on to other ports.

All of the trade between this Middle Eastern Arab–Muslim world and East Asia continued until the time of the Portuguese, which began in the last decade of the fifteenth century. These trading traditions also helped to spread Islam into present-day Indonesia and the Malay Peninsula as well as to solidify the spice-trading networks. Prior to the Crusades, European views about spice-growing areas of the world were mostly founded on tales and rumour. The historian Paul Freedman notes that, as far back as the seventh century, Europeans believed that pepper in India grew on trees 'guarded' by serpents that would bite and poison anyone who attempted to gather the spice. The only way to harvest pepper, they thus concluded, was to burn the trees, an act that would drive the snakes underground. This also helped to explain the long-held misperception that peppercorns were black as a result of burning trees. Until about 1500, people thought that black and white pepper were separate plants. One fourteenth-century monk wrote that black pepper came from the south side of the Caucasus Mountains where they grow in the hottest sunshine.

In 1226 a cookbook entitled *Kitab el-Tabih* appeared, describing 159 recipes for 'meats, poultry, fish, vegetables, dairy products and sweets'. Authored by Mohamed ben el Hassan el Baghdadi, this classic work outlined the herbs and spices used in Arab cooking. Among the spices saffron, coriander, cumin, ginger and cardamom were nutmeg, pepper, cinnamon and cloves. Hassan el Baghdadi also described the use of perfumed liquids such as rosewater and orange-flower water as well as pomegranates and the use of lemon and honey. Such an array of flavourings would have been overpowering to the mind and mouth of a European person living many degrees of latitude to the north in comparison with their usual diet. This cookbook was a testament to the established role of spices in the Arab world of the Middle East, which they had played for centuries.

The Crusades – the West's largely military response to its desire to free the Holy Land from Islamic influence – became a focal point in the history of spices in the twelfth and thirteenth centuries. As a result of the Crusades, the West experienced a religious revival that strengthened the power of the popes in Rome and also created an increase in self-awareness and a new confidence among Europeans. When the Crusaders ventured south-east to the Holy Land, they found a people and culture that were far more advanced than their own in terms of ideas and technology. Over time the Arab and Muslim numerical system had been derived from Indian mathematics, their astronomy from the Babylonians, philosophy from the Greeks which, along with Arab advances in business organization and nautical know-ledge, helped the West advance into the Renaissance and lead the way to the Scientific Revolution. However they were also bent on spreading *dar al-islam*, the house or domain of Islam and achieving that through *dar al-harb*, the domain of war.

When, at the end of the First Crusade in 1099, the Crusaders entered and conquered the Holy Land, the thou-sands of pilgrims who came with and after them witnessed first hand wondrous new ways of life in Syria and Palestine. Merchants in Venice and Genoa were promised landing rights

An exaggerated view of a cinnamon merchant from a 15th-century Italian manuscript. If cinnamon ever grew this large, legends about birds carrying the cinnamon to line their nests would be difficult to imagine.

to set up trading centres, where metals, wool and clothing from Europe were exchanged for spices, fruits and jewellery. Over the next century, while the Crusades continued, European eating habits slowly began to change. Pepper, nutmeg, cloves and cardamom entered the diet of the Crusaders, at the same time that other tantalizing foodstuffs such as figs, dates, almonds, lemons and oranges migrated north to European tables.

For Europeans of this era, spices were used both as a medicine and in the preparation of foods. One of the myths about spices was that they were used to preserve meats, but this idea has been mostly discarded for a number of reasons. Foremost among these was the fact that there was an abundance of meat in the medieval West, with animals routinely being killed, prepared, cooked and eaten, thus obviating the need for preserving. Secondly, spices are not particularly useful as a preservative. Salting, smoking or drying meat is much more effective, with salt being an excellent preservative that was readily available.

Over time, spices came to be related both to medicine and food consumption. This was specifically in terms of their relation to bodily fluids or the humours of dry, wet, hot and cold. 'Hot' spices, for instance, might be used in a sauce for a meat dish to counteract the 'wet' qualities of meat, thus enabling the body to remain healthy with a balance between the humours. Spices were considered to be either hot or dry. Pepper was rated as the hottest spice. An examination of medieval pharmacies reveals records that show pepper, cinnamon and ginger used in many medical prescriptions.

There are numerous medieval cookbooks that give an idea of the importance and multitude of spices in Europe at that time. One tells, for example, of a fifteenth-century Polish–Bavarian wedding that included the consumption of 205 pounds of cinnamon, 85 pounds of nutmeg, 105 of cloves and 386 of pepper. In another cookbook comprising some 200 recipes, 125 of them required cinnamon. In 1150 Saint Hildegard, the 'Sibyl of the Rhine', wrote a book about healing which praised the pharmaceutical qualities of nutmeg. Whoever received a nutmeg on New Year's Day and carried it in a pocket for a year could fall and never break a bone. Additionally, such a person would never suffer a stroke, or be burdened with haemorrhoids, scarlet fever or boils.

Nutmeg and mace were brought by Arab merchants to wealthy Constantinople in the sixth century and by the twelfth century nutmeg was mentioned in various European countries as far north as Scandinavia. Nutmeg was also used as an incense. In 1191, when Henry VI, a holy Roman emperor, was crowned in Rome, nutmeg was burned in the streets, along with other spices, for days before the coronation. According to Chaucer, people liked to put nutmeg in their beer. Today Bavarians use nutmeg in a root beer and at least two North American brewers, Dogfish Head and Samuel Adams, use nutmeg in selected beers. Nutmeg was also a vehicle for promoting sexism in the 1500s: Levinus Lennius, a Dutch physician, the author of *Nature's Secret Powers*, extolled the power of men over women by claiming that a nutmeg carried by a man would swell up and become juicy, pretty and more fragrant but one carried by a woman would wrinkle and become dry, dark, dirty and ugly. Once again the medieval idea of bodily fluids and humours play a role in these tales as man is endowed with better bodily qualities which make him strong and superior.

The Crusades also saw the importation of Arab cooks into the kitchens of Frankish high society in Middle Eastern cities such as Jerusalem and Acre. Music, dancing and literature were often linked with food at banquets during this time. The Crusading Franks also used spices such as cloves, cinnamon and saffron to demonstrate their great wealth. Ready-cooked foods were available in the markets of Jerusalem, a forerunner of the food stalls and markets of today. In 1194, when William I of Scotland paid a visit to his fellow monarch Richard I of England, he received a daily allotment of two

A medieval print of a nutmeg. After Europe discovered the nutmeg it became fashionable to carry strings of the nut around the neck accompanied by a grater.

pounds of pepper and four pounds of cinnamon. As to cloves, traditional herbal books claimed that a man who lost his potency could regain it with sweet milk embedded with three grams of crushed clove. In Moluccan folklore, villagers treated blossoming clove trees like pregnant women. No man

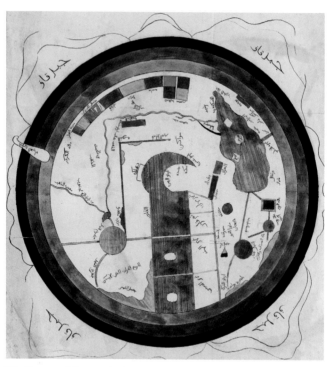

Islamic map of the world by Al-Qazuini, *c.* 1032. North is at the bottom, as is fairly common to early maps made in Europe and the Islamic world. West is to the right with Rome as a black square and Constantinople as a circle.

could approach them wearing a hat, no noise could be made near them and no light or fire could be carried past them at night for fear they would not bear fruit. Some Moluccans still plant a clove tree at the birth of a child, with the belief that if the tree flourishes, so will the child. A clove tree was considered to be so hot that nothing could grow under it. Even a pitcher of water left near cloves would evaporate in less than two days. In recent times in the East Indies some native inhabitants put cloves in their nostrils and between their lips so that demons would not enter their bodies.

A 16th-century woodcut depicting the gathering of cinnamon.

Besides being used in ceremonies and presented as gifts, spices were also collected as valued objects. At meals for the wealthy, spices were passed around the table on a gold or silver tray. This 'spice platter' may have contained sections with different spices that guests would put over their food, which may have already been flavoured with spices. At times food for the wealthy would be buried under layers of spices, in a medieval version of the 'conspicuous consumption' of today. Spices were also consumed in wine.

The rise of Venice and Genoa as ports, sea powers and conduits of the spice trade may have been a gift of geography and a strongly evolving merchant class located in well-situated places between northern Europe and the Middle East. Traders from Venice, on the Adriatic Sea, could sail or row south-east down the Mediterranean to Acre, the seaport long known as the 'key to Palestine' on the coast of present-day Israel and then move goods overland to Jerusalem. By the twelfth and thirteenth centuries, Europe was experiencing great economic growth. Now the West had goods such as textiles and metals that could be traded for the spices of the East. The marketplace at the foot of the Rialto Bridge in Venice saw the Lombards, Florentines and Germans dealing in a new world of banking, international finance and trade, the headquarters of which replaced the meat-packing and fish-sorting buildings by the famous span. The Germans brought their linen to trade and, after the discovery of silver mines in Saxony and elsewhere, bartered this precious metal for spices that eventually made their way north to influence the eating habits of Germany and other parts of Europe. Had there not been a demand in China and the Indian Ocean world for silver coin, the history of the spice trade might have taken a different turn. Additionally, merchants in Flanders and England brought copper and woollen cloth to the markets in exchange for pepper, cinnamon, cloves, nutmeg and ginger. Eastern spices were brought into Western Europe by sea, with Bruges, in Flanders, evolving as a major port. First the Genoese and later the Venetians would sail out of the Mediterranean, call at Lisbon and then proceed north into the English Channel east to Bruges.

The spices that came out of the East over the Indian Ocean usually were unloaded at the Straits of Ormuz on the Persian Gulf or at Aden on the south-eastern corner of

Arabia. More often than not, the spices were carried on the backs of camels. These 'ships of the desert' set off from Mecca and Medina, heading up the Arabian Peninsula to Cairo, Alexandria or Acre. The route from Ormuz either went west on camels to the Black Sea or east over water to Aleppo or other ports nearby, then on to Cyprus and west to Europe.

Although operating on the Ligurian coast side of the Italian 'boot', the Genoese had an equal footing with Venice in trade along the coast of Israel, as well as in Acre and, further north, Tyre, in Lebanon. They had been very helpful in supporting the Crusaders and thus enjoyed inroads into the spice trade. The competition between the two cities remained strong and eventually Venice and Genoa went to war with each other, but profit prevailed in the end and the trading continued. Over time Venice replaced Constantinople (present-day Istanbul) as a major trading centre. Not only were the Venetians getting various goods from northern Europe but also wine, oil, honey, wax, cotton, wool and hides from Eastern Europe. While Venice's traders still ventured east to retrieve spices, they were less dependent on going in that direction to obtain the products that came to them naturally as denizens of a trading centre.

An interesting aspect of the East–West spice trade was that traders from Europe needed to have someone based in Cairo, Tyre, Acre or Aleppo (in Syria) that they could trust, usually a relative. The Venetians were particularly good at setting up these family partnerships, in which one relation lived in the Levant. Confronted with the Arab and Muslim trading networks that had existed for centuries and had their own 'trust' systems, the Europeans had to learn to set up similar enterprises.

The trading system was a long, drawn-out process from beginning to end. The French historian Fernand Braudel,

胡
椒

Ming painting of black pepper, mid-17th century. Pepper was grown in north-west China and called *melluzhi* by the Chinese. The pepper leaves curl up at night and cover the berries and then unfurl in the morning.

considering the East–West spice trade, wrote in *The Perspective of the World*: 'One has only to think how many times a sack of pepper from India, or a sack of cloves from the East Indies, must have been handled before it reached a ship, first in Aleppo, then in Venice and finally in Nuremberg.'

While the Europeans viewed spices as exotic, they also saw them in a religious context. These fragrant commodities not only came from far-away places such as India and the Moluccas, but they were also from a fabled world. In his book *Tastes of Paradise,* Wolfgang Schivelbusch writes:

> Pepper was envisioned by Europeans growing in a bamboo forest, on a plain near Paradise. Ginger and cinnamon were hauled in by Egyptian fishermen casting nets into the Floodwaters of the Nile, which in turn had carried them straight from Paradise. The aroma of spices was believed to be a breath wafted from Paradise over the human world. No medieval writer could envision Paradise without the smell or taste of spices. Whether the poetically described gardens served saints or lovers, the atmosphere was inevitably infused with the rare, intoxicating fragrance of cinnamon, nutmeg, ginger and cloves. On the basis of such fantasies, it was possible for lovers and friends to exchange certain spices as pledges of their relationship.

A simple look at many early maps gives a second-millennium viewer a window onto what someone in the Middle Ages saw as the relationship between the known and unknown worlds and the belief that both paradise (and hell) existed at some other, unknown, but identified space on that map.

Spices were an integral part of the growth of the European economy. Values were relative. A pound of nutmeg, in the Germany of 1393, was worth seven oxen.

In the eleventh century ships at Billingsgate paid part of their toll to King Ethelred in pepper. Peppercorns were accepted as a payment for rents and taxes and some European towns kept their accounts in pepper. In England some farm workers could pay their rent with one pound of pepper, about three weeks' wages for that profession. Out of this grew the custom of handing over a single peppercorn as a token for a relationship of tenancy. This led to the expression 'a peppercorn rent'. When Prince Charles took possession of his Duchy of Cornwell in 1973, a pound of pepper was part of the tribute he received.

Standards of living had improved after the Crusades. Aside from Bruges, Genoa and Venice, cities such as Nuremberg, Augsburg, Bordeaux and Antwerp developed their own trade monopolies. In the late twelfth century, the Guild of Pepperers, a social and religious fraternity of wholesale merchants and bankers, was set up in London. The group merged with a spicers' organization and eventually evolved into the Worshipful Company of Grocers (members bought and sold 'in gross', hence the noun 'grosser' and then 'grocer'), the community that managed the trade in spices for the English monarch. In the early seventeenth century, some members of the grocers' guild were granted a royal charter to form their own guild, the Worshipful Society of Apothecaries (or pharmacists), a group that continued the link between spices and medicine – and also challenged the long-held hegemony of the Royal College of Physicians.

The two greatest travellers of the early modern world, the Venetian Marco Polo (1254–1324) and the Moroccan Ibn Battuta (1304–1368/1377), are a study in contrasts. Ibn Battuta travelled much further than his European counterpart, from West Africa to South and East Asia, in what would constitute

Marco Polo's travels across Central Asia into China were not as extensive as those completed by Ibn Battuta, who travelled more miles, but did not experience the level of culture shock that Polo did.

40 modern nations. Marco Polo was literally 'a stranger in a strange land', crossing a wide Mongol landscape and spending decades in China. Ibn Battuta conducted most of his travels in a Muslim world or Dar al-Islam. He mostly covered the proceedings of the educated, cultural class, writing about subjects that would interest those people. In at times a florid, fanciful style, he portrayed a world where the values were the same as his, but where regional customs were different. When Ibn Battuta got to China he experienced culture shock, noting: 'Every time I left my house, I saw reprehensible things. I was so disturbed that I stayed home most of the time, only going out when necessary.' But later he altered this view, writing, 'China is the safest and pleasantest country in the world for the traveller.'

Marco Polo has given us an accurate description of medieval China and other parts of Asia towards the end of

As spices such as pepper, cloves and cinnamon travelled westward from South and East Asia, buyers needed to be wary of adulterated sacks.

the thirteenth century. While writing his account in a Genoese prison during the Venice–Genoa war, he limned an exotic world that was totally new. Marco Polo had started his journey going east to China, where he remained for almost twenty years. On his return trip he took a southern route through South East Asia, India and Persia. He described the amount of pepper that came into Chinese ports as a hundred times greater than that which came to Alexandria from India. He reported on plants such as cassia and ginger and described different foods and drinks that contained spices. In the city of Hangchow (Hangzhou), south-west of Shanghai, an official told him that 10,000 pounds of pepper were brought into that city every day. He also described, on his return home, the plantings of cloves, pepper and nutmeg in the East Indies.

Ibn Battuta started his trip in various ports in Arabia such as Aden. He then visited East Africa, where he described some eating habits he saw in Mogadishu:

> They eat rice cooked with ghee . . . on top they set dishes of *kushan*. These are relishes composed of chicken, meat, fish and vegetables. In one dish they serve green bananas in fresh milk, in another yogurt with pickled lemon, bunches of pepper pickled in vinegar and salt, green ginger and mangos.

The Muslim explorer was one of the first observers to record information about the cinnamon trade of Ceylon:

> Puttalam [north of present-day Colombo] the capital, is a small and pretty town, surrounded by a wall and palisades. The whole of the coast near here is covered with the trunks of cinnamon trees brought down by the rivers. They are collected in mounds on the seashore. People from Coromandel and Malabar take them away without paying for them, but they give the sultan cloth and such in exchange.

The writer also described a meal in Kerala, the most south-western state of India in the centre of India's pepper-growing area:

A beautiful slave girl, dressed in silk, places before the king the bowls containing the individual dishes. With a large bronze ladle she places a ladleful of rice on the platter; pours ghee over it, and adds preserved peppercorns, green ginger, preserved lemons and mangos. The diner takes a mouthful of rice and then a little of these conserves. When the helping of rice is all eaten, she ladles out some more, and serves a dish of chicken, again eaten with rice.

In his book *The Spice Route*, John Keay points out that Ibn Battuta gets some of his botanicals mixed up when he writes, 'As for the fruit of the clove, it is none other than the nutmeg; and the flower which is formed within it [the nut] is mace. I have seen all this and been witness to it.'

Because the writings of Ibn Battuta were done mostly within and intended for readers of the Islamic world, spices and spice routes were already known there, so he was not imparting any new facts. Marco Polo, on the other hand, provided a narrative that brought new and fascinating information to the West, thus whetting its denizens' collective appetite for spices.

In the early modern world of the fourteenth and fifteenth centuries and during the height of Mameluke power in North Africa and the rise of the Ottoman Empire out of Turkey, the European lake known as the Mediterranean became an Ottoman body of water. It was not until 1571, at the naval battle of Lepanto, off western Greece, when the Ottoman domination of trade on the Mediterranean ended. However, that control of the Mediterranean by the Ottomans motivated Western Europe to find a new way to bring spices to their markets. The Western Age of Exploration was dawning.

3
The Age of Exploration

Thus to the Eastern wealth through storms we go,
But now, the Cape once doub'led, fear no more;
A constant trade-wind will securely blow,
And gently lay us on the spicy shore.
Annus Mirabilis, John Dryden

The 'Age of Exploration', a West European expression, involved the nations of coastal/continental Europe and the British Isles. From the late fifteenth to the nineteenth century, Portugal, Spain, the Netherlands, England and, to a lesser degree, France and Denmark, competed for the market in spices in two areas of the world, South Asia and South East Asia. These countries' efforts to capture one or more parts of the spice trade were global, involving both the western and eastern hemispheres. There were also attempts to find northern and southern routes to the lands of spices. In the sixteenth and seventeenth centuries, as nations competed, the quest for spices evolved into what can truly be viewed as the 'First World War'.

In the millennium before Europe encountered South Asia, the south-west – or Malabar – coast of India flourished as a fecund realm of spices and scents – the first key to unlocking the story of this age of converging cultures. At least 500 years before Europe ventured eastwards, Christians, Muslims, Jews and Hindus formed the basis of a society in Kerala, on the Malabar coast. It was here that 'black gold' grew as a vine-gripping plant that attached itself to trees and formed bunches of small green buds called pepper. The pepper grows in this south-western part of the Western Ghats, the mountain range that runs north to south astride the Arabian Sea. It is a rainforest land of waterfalls, lakes, apes and elephants, where soft mists fill the air; in short, an ideal atmosphere for the pepper to grow. One spice trader described it as 'beautiful and peaceful'. The green bunches are picked, separated from the stem and allowed to dry in the sun until they shrivel and turn black. Also grown in south-western India were ginger, turmeric and cardamom, all staples of the Indian diet. However, pepper was the sovereign spice that was known in the Arab world to the north-west and to traders from East Asia centuries before the Europeans came at the tail end of the fifteenth century.

In South East Asia, the position of the Spice Islands (formerly the Moluccas, present-day Maluku Islands) is the second key to the Age of Exploration. These are a small group of volcanic land masses in present-day Indonesia, south of the Philippines, east of Borneo and Java, north of Australia and west of New Guinea. The archipelago includes five islands – Ternate, Tidore, Motir (Moti), Makian (Machian) and Bachan (Bacan) – which are the original sources of the clove. The source of nutmeg and mace was the Banda Islands. Larger Indonesian islands such as Bali and Timor also had spices, but nutmeg and cloves were limited to those areas mentioned above. Europe got a first-hand account of these islands and India from an Italian, Ludovico Varthema, in his *Itinerary* of 1510. According to Donald F.

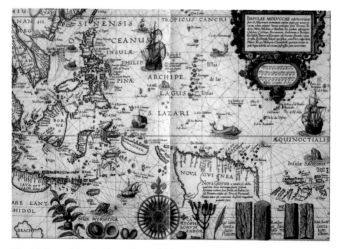

The Molucca Islands (from *Insviae Molvccae* by Peter Plancius) The original
source of nutmeg and cloves, the name of these islands, known as Moluku
to the Arabs, meant 'land of many kings', an apt description, since there
are over 17,000 Molucca Islands. Note the nutmeg and cloves at the
bottom of the map.

Lach in *Asia in the Making of Europe*, Varthema went to the
East through the Levant, learned Arabic and acknowledged
Islam. He left Venice in 1502 and arrived in India in 1504,
coming into Calicut (now Kozhikode) early in 1505. Here he
devotes most of his writing to the pepper-growing and culture of the people in this Malabar region of West India.
Subsequently he rounded the southern tip of India at Cape
Comorin and ventured up the east coast of India. Lach
writes that it is at this point that the Italian's *Itinerary*
becomes vague and his descriptions inaccurate. However,
later in his journal he notices the nutmeg tree and gives a
description of the clove tree, which indicates that he might
have been in the Moluccas. Varthema returned to Europe
from the west coast of India on a Portuguese ship and
ended up in Rome, where his travels were published.

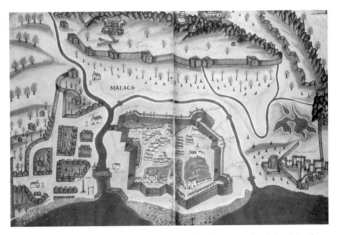

Malacca: Malacca was vital to linking the Indian Ocean to the Spice Islands. Located on the lower western side of the Malay Peninsula astride the narrow strait bearing its name, Malacca was historically a major trading hub linking China with the West. Both the Portuguese and the Dutch have controlled it.

As with India, there was an extensive spice-trading network throughout this area for centuries. Spices were bought with Chinese silks, Indian cottons, Arabian coffee and African ivory. The distances involved were vast, considering that Indonesia, south of Singapore, is about 3,000 miles from top to bottom, roughly the distance from Los Angeles to New York City.

As the trade in spices intensified, this became a significant region for the Portuguese, Dutch, English, Spanish and, later, French and Danish. By the middle of the sixteenth century, as a result of the Portuguese trade route around Africa to India and the Moluccas, and the Spanish moving west into the Pacific from Mexico through Manila, the West covered the middle latitudes of the major world oceans. These subtropical lanes of the sea were sailed by the two Iberian powers and caused the English, in particular, to seek a northern route to the lands of spices.

The Portuguese Enter the East

This historical and large-scale encounter between the worlds of Europe and Asia begins with the Portuguese in 1498. Imagine visiting a new culture where you have no knowledge of the language or the culture of the people you encounter. In our modern world of instant translation of languages and cross-cultural knowledge, as well as rapid movement from place to place by land, sea and air, the enormity of this may be difficult to grasp. In 1498, when the Portuguese explorer Vasco da Gama arrived at the port of Calicut on the western Malabar coast of India, he was had the enormous challenge of acquainting himself with the nature of the world in which he found himself.

This quest for knowledge and power continued between 1589 and 1622, as the Carreira da India ('course to India') route operated from Lisbon, down to the east coast of Africa at Mozambique and on to the west Indian ports of Cochin in the south and Goa to the north.

When da Gama arrived in India, it was 28 years before the Mogul conquest of this subcontinent. In Calicut and Kerala, the Hindus were the ruling class. However, Muslims, Arabs and Persians, who did not look favourably upon outsiders, controlled the export trade. Da Gama and some of his crew met the Calicut Hindu leader (or 'Samuri'), who had been told that King Manoel of Portugal was very rich. Da Gama gave the Samuri leader some trinkets such as striped cloth, scarlet hoods, hats, strings of coral, washbasins, sugar, oil and honey. The Samuri, who received this 'bounty' while sitting on his throne chewing on betel nuts and spitting the juice into a golden spittoon, was very disappointed with the gifts and this gave his Muslim advisers the opportunity to characterize da Gama and his crew as nothing more than marauders.

Goa: this land-locked island became the centre of the Portuguese spice world on the Malabar coast of India as well as its only shipbuilding port in Asia.

The Portuguese were then taken to a Hindu temple where da Gama, seeing a statue that resembled the Virgin Mary (which he later sprinkled with water), assumed the structure was a different type of Catholic Church. On their way back to the ship, the export traders detained da Gama and his crew and held them for days. Da Gama was almost assassinated, but his group was saved by the Samuri. A legend from this encounter was that before da Gama left India he asked for a pepper stalk to take home for replanting. The Samuri's advisers were outraged, but the ruler calmly told da Gama, 'You can take our pepper, but you will never be able to take our rains.' After a few months, da Gama was able to secure some peppercorns and gems and he headed west to Portugal. His trip was not easy, resulting in the loss of crew members, mostly to scurvy, and the need to dismantle one of his ships on the East African coast. After other stops for

water and food, da Gama's ships rounded Cape Horn, with two of the vessels separately making it back to Lisbon after an absence of over two years.

Looking back on da Gama's meeting with the Samuri, it is hard to believe that the Portuguese were so naive as to expect to gain shiploads of pepper for such paltry gifts. After all, there had been legends about the Eastern world known by Europeans for centuries. Even if they did not believe all of the tales of Eastern riches, the travellers should have been better prepared for an exchange of a valued product such as black pepper. Time would prove that only silver, gold and other valuable commodities would suffice for an exchange of spices.

Da Gama realized that the Portuguese would not have success in India and elsewhere unless they broke the monopoly of the Arab, Muslim and Persian merchants. These groups had controlled the export trade for centuries in the Indian Ocean, and Calicut was the centre of it all where east and

Noble Portuguese in India. A 16th-century Indian artist's depiction of a Portuguese official and his followers on the Malabar coast of India.

west trading met. In March 1500 a Portuguese fleet set out for India with thirteen fully armed ships and 1,200 men. Under the leadership of Pedro Alvares Cabral, the expedition headed south-west to find the point of sail that would allow them to sail east around the Cape of Good Hope. In doing so they came very close to land and ended up disembarking on Brazilian soil, thus becoming the first Europeans to do so. Was this a planned attempt to find a new continent or an accident? Historians are not sure. Cabral sent one ship back to Portugal to announce the news. A horrible storm separated and wrecked some of the fleet as it left Brazil. The seven surviving ships met in East Africa and then went on to Calicut, arriving within six months of leaving Lisbon.

The Portuguese were received by the Hindu Samuri, who allowed them to build a factory. To repay this debt to the Samuri, Cabral seized a Muslim ship in order to transport an elephant to the Samuri as a gift. The Muslim merchants retaliated by storming the factory and killing some fifty Portuguese. Cabral then burned ten of their ships with their crews and bombarded Calicut with all of his guns. This was the first act of war against the Muslims, and the Hindu Samuri was angered by the damage done to his city. The Portuguese left and moved south, and then later went back north up the coast, where word of their firepower had spread. In both places they met docile leaders and were able to load pepper and other spices onto their ships and head home. Merchants and investors from all over Europe descended on Lisbon to support the Portuguese and their trading ventures. Meanwhile, in Venice the news was not good. The overland trade routes from India that had given 'the Queen of the Adriatic' a European monopoly for centuries were damaged.

The Portuguese successes were to continue, although they became bloody cross-cultural encounters. Vasco da Gama returned to Calicut after Cabral as a last-minute replacement for the discoverer of Brazil, which made Cabral resentful of da Gama and forced him into retirement. Da Gama returned with more pepper and later Afonso de Albuquerque firmly established Portuguese dominance in India with the building of a fort at Cochin.

Between 1503 and 1540, the Portuguese supplied Europe with most of its pepper. By 1540 there were over 10,000 people of European descent living on the west coast of India. Although Portugal had established a spice base in Asia, it was unable to capture the Muslim ports at the entrance to the Red Sea. If the Portuguese had been successful here, they could have dominated much of the spice trade moving from east to west by land and sea. Although Portugal was the principal supplier of spices in the northern hemisphere at this time, its inhabitants did not take to spicy dishes as easily as the South

OCOVERNADOR AFFONÇO EIALBOQVERQVE·SVÇEDEO NA INDIA
A DOM·FRANCISCO·EIAL·ME[...] IDA. EM NOVEMBRO·DE
509·TOMOV4DAS VEZE S [...] [...]DADEEIGOA·EASEIMALA
ET EORV2EFFEZA·FORTALEZ [...]A·EICALECV·TEEDIA·PERCIA·EA0
ESTRETO·DE ORMVZ·E MAR·ROXO

Afonso de Albuquerque: the conqueror of Goa and the first Viceroy of the Portuguese empire in India, he was responsible for breaking the Muslim monopoly on the spice trade in the Indian Ocean. He also captured the vital port of Malacca in 1511 and the Straits of Ormuz four years later, which enabled control of the Persian Gulf.

Asian Indians who supplied them or the Portuguese who resided in India. However, over time, Portuguese dishes such as *Toucinho do Céu* (Bacon from Heaven) and almond cake used cinnamon. In pork dishes such as *Carne de Vinho e Alhos*, which is pork braised in white wine with herbs and orange wedges, cloves are used for additional flavour.

The Italians were European leaders in the use of spices during this period. Perhaps this was because of the east and west ports of Venice and Genoa that had a long tradition of importing spices. As early as the thirteenth and fourteenth centuries, cinnamon, cloves and pepper were used in spice mixtures. Jill Norman outlines the ingredients for 'Scappi's Spice Mix', produced by Bartolomeo Scappi, the cook to Pope Pius v in his *Opera dell'Arte del Cucinare*, an influential cookbook of the sixteenth century. This mix includes 24 cinnamon sticks, 1 ounce of cloves, ½ ounce of dried ginger and ½ ounce of nutmeg as well as ¼ ounce of grains of paradise (a West African plant that grows in large pods whose pungent seeds are used for flavouring), ¼ ounce of saffron and ½ ounce of brown sugar. The book recommends that the cinnamon sticks be broken up and all other ingredients ground into a fine powder which should be stored in a jar and would keep for three to four months.

During the remainder of the sixteenth century, the Portuguese continued to move to the east, seeking out the Spice Islands and the spice-trading routes of East and South East Asia, an attempt that proved successful. At the south-west tip of the Malay Peninsula, the Portuguese captured Malacca, a vital chokepoint to the straits that bear its name and the entry to South East Asia and the Spice Islands. The Portuguese continued to have success in the spice realm by force of arms, but they also realized that many of the native land-based powers in Asia did not concern themselves with the sea, or else they were engaged in rivalries with other land-based regions and kingdoms. This allowed the Iberians to flourish on the sea. It should be noted that the dominant Muslim trading networks the Portuguese entered in South and East Asia continued with a great deal of success. The Portuguese did not control the trade in spices; they merely got their share. Additionally, at their base in Macao and for their trading with the Chinese,

Earth Protected by Juniper and Juno. This 16th-century tapestry woven in silver, gold, silk and wool shows the Portuguese King and his Queen displaying their domain over their Portuguese overseas empire. Note the small gold coloured circles and squares denoting Portuguese presence in Africa and South Asia.

the Chinese dictated the terms of trade. Along the Malabar coast of India, the Portuguese only controlled about 5 per cent of the spice trade. As for pepper, they only procured 10 per cent of that trade. Profits were good for the merchants in Portugal who invested in the spice trade, but the Estados da India venture of the Portuguese crown was a losing

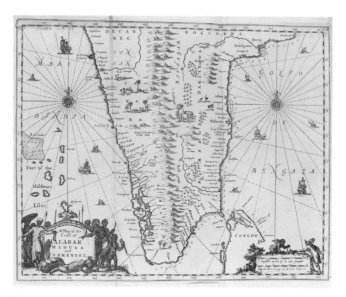

An 18th-century map of India showing the Malabar coast (a source of black pepper) on the left, the Coromandel Coast on the right, and Madurai in southern India.

proposition. The Portuguese did gain profit from their sea voyages to India, but most of the European profits were made by those merchants who took their spices from the overland Red Sea route.

Nevertheless, the world was changing, and east to west, as the historian C. R. Boxer wrote, the Portuguese empire gathered the following products: gold from Guinea, southeast Africa and Sumatra; the sugar of Madeira, São Tomé and Brazil; pepper from Malabar and Indonesia; mace and nutmeg from Banda; cloves from Ternate, Tidore and Amboina; cinnamon from Ceylon; gold, silks and porcelain from China; silver from Japan; horses from Persia and Arabia; and cotton textiles from India. In *The Lusiads*, the late sixteenth-century epic verse of Portuguese exploration by Luís de Camões, the poet writes of the glory of his compatriots' venture to the east:

> This celebrated coast of India, as you see, continues to run southward till it ends in Cape Comorin, once Cape Core, facing Taprobana or Ceylon. Everywhere along these shores Portuguese soldiers still to come will win victories, lands, and cities, and here, for long ages they will make their abode.

The dream of ongoing glory was to fade. It was during the seventeenth century that Portuguese dominance would be eroded by the Dutch and the English as well as by local leaders who began to assert themselves in a more dynamic fashion. By the end of the 1600s, Portugal had lost most of its Asian bases.

The Spanish Connect East and West

After the voyages of Christopher Columbus of 1492, the Spanish focused their efforts on the western hemisphere – in Mexico and Central and South America. However, this did not mean that the Spanish crown did not have an interest in the spice trade. The major motivation for Columbus's voyage, in fact, was to locate this Eastern spice trade. Later, when another Spanish explorer, Ferdinand Magellan, had circumnavigated the globe, he explored the Philippines where he met his death. The Spanish searched the Philippines for spices and gold but did not find much of interest. However, there were no Portuguese or Dutch there, and they were near the Spice Islands, so they established settlements. Spain then started a trade route, called the 'Manila galleon', between the eponymous Philippine city, its major settlement in the island nation, and Acapulco in Mexico. It is known that some cinnamon crossed the Pacific to Mexico along this route, but most of the spices that reached the Americas from Spain came from the traditional itinerary west across the Indian Ocean to the Atlantic, rather than the more direct, but very long, way across the Pacific.

When Magellan circled the earth, he had a mandate from the Spanish crown to find spices or to negotiate for them. On board his flagship was Antonio Pigafetta, who imparted information about spices as the expedition moved through the Spice Islands. He wrote that 'the best cinnamon that can be found' on an island grew on a tall tree with leaves similar to the laurel and branches 'as thick as fingers' whose bark was collected twice a year. The nutmeg tree was like the walnut and had a bright red cover of mace that surrounded the nut. Since cloves were considered the most exotic and

A cinnamon tree, depicted in the 15th-century German manuscript *Gart der Gesundheit* (Garden of Health). The cinnamon tree has been said to live over 200 years.

valuable spice, Pigafetta spent a great deal of time describing them: their height and thickness (as 'tall and as big around as a man'), the shape of their leaves, the colour of the bark and the cloves themselves. As mentioned earlier, the cloves grew in very specific locations in the mountains of the five islands where they are extant. Pigafetta wrote that each day a cloud descended around the plants and, because of the moisture and cooler temperatures, 'the cloves became perfect'. When Magellan's leaderless ship returned to Spain, it was laden with valuable cloves. Unfortunately, a second vessel of this famous expedition never made it back because it was so overloaded with spices.

The Spanish crown was not satisfied with obtaining spices second hand. They set out to look for new spices in the Philippines and their colonies in Latin America or to consider transplanting spice plants in the lands they controlled. Some variations of the premier spices were eventually found in the Philippines, where local varieties of cinnamon, pepper and nutmeg grew. Cinnamon was so plentiful that it was used as a fuel. Wild pepper grew but was not cultivated. However, despite some attempts at cultivation, there was no significant development of spices such as nutmeg and cloves. On the other side of the world, Columbus thought he had found cinnamon (not true) and pepper (a long pepper found around Panama and Colombia which, because of its strong scent, was thought to be more healthy). A variation of cinnamon was found near Quito, Ecuador, and was brought to Europe, but it had neither taste nor aroma so perhaps was not cinnamon at all but merely wishful thinking on the part of the sailors.

Transplanting the spices was a significant undertaking for the Spanish in their new American colonies, known as 'New Spain'. The Spanish were not only interested in spices

Ternate, an island in eastern Indonesia, was the original source of cloves.
The island was controlled by Islamic sultans, who became extremely rich
selling cloves to buyers from both east and west.

as a food stimulus but also as a medicine. They had learned
much from the Arab/Muslim conquest of southern Spain
after 711. The Arabs had done a great deal of experimenta-
tion with plants and transplanting over the centuries, and this
quest for knowledge regarding the use of spices and other
plants in medicine took hold in the Spanish Empire. In the
1550s, New Spain was given the exclusive right (or *asiento*) to
plant the seeds of black pepper, cloves, cinnamon and ginger.
Of these only ginger was able to take root and prosper. Later,
in the seventeenth century, the planting of cloves was
attempted, but this endeavour was also unsuccessful. It was
difficult to duplicate the conditions of those five Spice
Islands where moisture and cooler temperatures filled the
air. Ginger (*Zingiber officinale*) was one success story, however,

not only in New Spain, but also in and around Seville and at the gardens of the Alcazar, the royal palace of Spain. The southern part of Spain, after the eighth century and before the expulsion of the Moors in 1492, was dominated by Arab cooking. This of course continued. When chilli peppers arrived from the Americas they were, over time, used in different ways. The peppers were eaten roasted over coals, boiled in liquid, prepared with salt, oil and vinegar, or dried and pounded into a soft powder. They were also used as a substitute for black pepper.

Dutch Competition and Dominance

During the sixteenth century, Portugal's grasp was far-reaching on the world scene, extending from Lisbon to Brazil to Japan, with the capital a major centre of Western Europe. However, this control was about to be challenged by the Dutch. While Portugal was ascending to European leadership of the Eastern spice trade, the Dutch were dominating the trade on the rivers of Europe and in the Baltic Sea. It was clear that the Low Country denizens had a keen commercial and seafaring sense, but what factors propelled them to sail the oceans to the East?

In the mid-sixteenth century, the Netherlands, or Low Countries, comprised a complex set of states and towns, loosely federated in seventeen provinces dominated by the Catholic king of Spain. There had been some armed resistance against Spain in 1566 by Calvinist Protestants, and by 1579 this conflict had been resolved with the Union of Utrecht, in which the southern Netherlands remained loyal to Spain and the seven northern provinces, centred on Amsterdam, became the Dutch Union. By 1602 a company was formed to pursue world trade. In the 80 years that followed, this small confederation rose to the apex of the global trading world. Already seaborne in the Baltic and on Europe's rivers, the union would undergo a transformation and expansion that would extend around the globe. The initial Dutch move into the oceans was not in the eastern but in the western hemisphere, where it centred on Brazil. One expedition to that South American nation in 1593 brought to Amsterdam a shipload of gold and ivory. The Netherlands controlled almost two-thirds of the European–Brazilian trade by 1621, the same year the Dutch West India Company was formed to regulate trade.

Dutch ventures into Asia began with Dutch citizens who had sailed with the Portuguese to Asia. They had gained valuable knowledge about the spice trade routes. By 1594 the Dutch launched ships to Indonesia. Two years later a few returned with a modest cargo of pepper, which more than covered the cost of the expedition. In 1598 another fleet set out, returning less than fifteen months later with a costly cargo of spices. In the holds of the returning ships were 600,000 pounds of pepper, 250,000 pounds of cloves and lesser amounts of mace and nutmeg. One Dutchman exclaimed: 'So long as Holland has been Holland, such richly laden ships have never been seen.' The total profit for the voyage was 400 per cent.

Trade now intensified as fourteen fleets with 65 ships set out for the East Indies in 1601. However, there was a fundamental problem with these earlier voyages. Each of the fleets and ships that left Holland was funded individually or by political units of either North or South Holland. The Union of Utrecht had not solidified the economic interests of Holland. In the Spice Islands, individual Dutch ships in the same port were vying for the same spices, a situation that was far from ideal. When ships and fleets returned to the various ports of Holland before 1602, the profits, or the loss of money for failed voyages, were not shared by all. Individual companies were going into bankruptcy. After much strain, dissent and argument among the many factions, the end of 1602 saw the birth of the United East India Company, or the voc (Vereenigde Oost-Indische Compagnie), more commonly known as the Dutch East India Company.

The unified Dutch economic compass was now pointed directly at Asia and, for the most part, success came the nation's way. The Dutch were very straightforward in their trading, using silver coin – rather than Vasco da Gama trinkets – to purchase spices. In 1605 the Portuguese lost the Spice Islands to the Dutch, in 1641 Malacca fell, in 1656 Colombo was in Dutch hands, in 1658 Ceylon and the cinnamon trade was Dutch and in 1662 Cochin went to the voc. The dominant trade in spices had a new leader. One Dutch ditty of the day went:

> Wherever profit leads us,
> To every sea and shore,
> For love of gain,
> The wide world's harbours we explore.

Concurrent with their many successes, the Dutch experienced hard lessons in cross-cultural learning. In the year after the voc was formed, the Dutch were in Ceylon seeking a way into the cinnamon trade when they were approached by the Singhalese Maharajah of Kandy, located east of Colombo in the centre of the island nation. The maharajah asked the East India traders to assist him in getting rid of the Portuguese. The Singhalese leader was angry that the Portuguese had taken over the productive coastal cinnamon areas and sent him inland. Meanwhile, the Dutch sailors, after a long time at sea eating salted beef, caught sight of some cows on the hillsides and longed for freshly cooked beef. An overture to buy the beasts was made to the Singhalese, who were horrified, since their religion held that the cows harboured the souls of their dead relatives. The Dutch leader did not take this seriously and allowed a few of the animals to be slaughtered, thinking that payment could be made after the fact. Not surprisingly, the Singhalese reacted badly, and relations between the two groups deteriorated. The Dutch had made another cultural error with the Sultan of Achin, at the northern tip of Sumatra, when they presented the Muslim leader with a greeting written on parchment made from pigskin. The convergence of cultures continued with more negative results.

A son of the Netherlands, Jan Huygen van Linschoten, sometimes referred to as the Dutch Marco Polo, illuminated the evolution and culture of the Dutch experience in Asia. He described the sixteenth-century spice world in writings called the *Itinerario*, or a journey or description of his travels. Later he wrote about the nature of the Dutch empire in editions also published in German and English in the seventeenth century. This merchant and explorer started working for the Portuguese in the last quarter of the 1500s and was sent to Goa on the coast of west India. Here he copied maps and other important information such as trading stations and resupply points of Portuguese trade, which were to prove extremely helpful to the Dutch. Linschoten also rendered detailed descriptions of spice trees and spice-growing areas. One portrayal of residents of a clove-growing area of the Moluccas includes mention of a drink with 'four drammes [of cloves] being drunke with Milk', a potable said to 'procure lust'. When initially published

Senior Merchant of the Dutch East Indian Company and his Wife Before Batavia (present day Jakarta) by Albert Cuyp, *c.* 1650. Anyone caught stealing spices in the Dutch spice empire faced the death penalty.

between 1579 and 1592, the *Itinerario* not only helped the development of the Dutch spice empire but also aided the English, who used the writings in their quest for spices.

In the next century the young Dutch minister François Valentijn ventured out to the Spice Islands, eventually reaching Ceylon. A keen observer of the world, Valentijn's record of the Dutch spice empire in Asia is one of the best written. His description of Ceylon as being shaped like a large ham precedes his vivid portrait of the cinnamon tree and the process of developing the spice:

> These trees sometimes grow very tall and sometimes medium. Their leaves are comparable to a citron leaf or to a laurel leaf in thickness and colour and the cinnamon leaf has three veins. The young leaves on first coming out are as red as scarlet and when broken in pieces smell much more like cloves than cinnamon. The tree has white

flowers which have a lovely and agreeable smell, from which come a fruit which is as big as an olive ... The tree grows wild like other jungle trees and is not valued any higher by the natives. This tree has a double bark, the outermost, which is not like cinnamon and which one peels with a knife, and the innermost which is the real cinnamon and is peeled with the curved edge of a knife first in a circle and then lengthwise, and laid to dry in the sun where they roll into each other, and are curled together as we generally see them ... There are three sorts of cinnamon here; first the fine, which is peeled from the young and middle-aged trees; the second, the coarse which comes from thicker and older trees; and the third, the wood or wild cinnamon, which is also found in Malabar and in other quarters. But the real cinnamon is found nowhere else except on this island.

As the Dutch tightened their control on the Spice Islands, their administration of the spice-growing process was a harsh and demanding one. In order to control the market in spices such as nutmeg and cloves, the Dutch only allowed the growth of a certain number of plants. This cultivation was strictly regulated, enabling the Dutch to control European markets in spices for a long period of time. However, the effect of this action on the native peoples growing the spices was damning. One example of this is found in the Banda Islands, the sole source of nutmeg and mace. The Dutch began trading here with the Bandanese, who initially were very agreeable to making a treaty with them – but were later just as willing to break that bond when the English and Portuguese appeared and wanted their share of nutmeg. This aggravated the Dutch to such an extent that they were forced to take strong measures. In 1615 it was

EUGENIA CARYOPHYLLATA, *Thunb.*

Eugenia caryophyllata. The clove was native to Ternate, an island in the East Indies.

declared in Holland that 'the Bandanese should be overpowered, the chiefs exterminated and chased away, and the land repopulated with heathens [slaves].'

The Dutch asked for a monopoly, it was refused by the Bandanese, a battle ensued and the Bandanese surrendered to Dutch sovereignty. However, the terms of the treaty were broken by the residents of Banda, and the Dutch proceeded to slaughter the natives. Slaves were brought in to replace the native population, and the Dutch tried to encourage their homebound citizens to colonize the islands.

These incursions on the indigenous populations were direct violations of cultural mores. One custom in the clove-growing islands was that a clove tree was planted for every baby born. If a clove tree was cut down, it might bring bad fortune to a child. The Dutch policies eventually allowed them to have major control of three of the premier spices in the East Indies. Of the trading islands in this region, first, cloves on Amboina, and then pepper on Ternate and Tidore preceded nutmeg as spices under Dutch control. So demanding were the colonists about the control of the spice markets that it was said that if there were too many spices entering the European market, 'mountains' of cinnamon and nutmeg would be burned in Amsterdam in order to maintain prices.

Like the Portuguese, whom they ran out of the Spice Islands, the Dutch never had any control of the trade in spices. The German historian and sociologist Andre Gunder Frank wrote that the Chinese and other East Asians ruled the seas. From the late seventeenth century onwards, European penetration was actually reversed. Other historians point out that the Portuguese and Dutch were able to make the inroads that they did because of local and regional power vacuums that they filled for short periods of time, playing one region off another. The Dutch, even with their colonies and full shares, got only a small part of the global trade in spices. Finally, and of no little importance, the Dutch were instrumental in bringing Asia into the world economy as no other people were. Asia and Europe were inextricably linked.

The English Evolve from Pirates to Players

The formation of the Dutch East India Company not only united the Dutch and allowed them to dominate the seas of Asia, but it also did great damage to the English by not permitting them to get a full share of the spice trade. However, there were some English successes along the way, including control over some of the Spice Islands for limited periods of time.

The first favourable outcomes occurred during Sir Francis Drake's circumnavigation of the world. In November 1579 he arrived at Ternate in the East Indies. Here he made a treaty with the Sultan Baabullah, buying a huge amount of cloves. After striking a reef and being delayed, Drake was able to continue west into the Indian Ocean. However, his ship, the *Golden Hind*, was forced to dump much of its cargo because it was overwhelmed with the weight of the spice. With the remaining spices and other precious cargo, Drake arrived back in England in late September 1580. The profit for the voyage was estimated at 4,600 per cent (£47 for each £1 invested). Because of Drake's success, Queen Elizabeth 1 was petitioned to sanction an expedition. In 1592 James Lancaster and George Raymond sailed from Plymouth, on England's south coast. Raymond's ship was lost, and Lancaster proceeded on to the East Indies, plundering Portuguese ships in the Straits of Malacca and establishing a British base on the north-western tip of Java in Bantam (near present-day Banten), the most important port in the spice trade from the sixteenth through to the eighteenth century. Stimulated by the founding of their own East India Company in 1600, the English continued their quest for spices. Despite this and other initiatives, the Dutch managed to keep the English at bay through much of the next century and, not surprisingly, some of these difficult situations increased the tension between the two nations.

The British had not been able to make significant inroads in the Spice Islands, and investors in the London-based East India Company were ready to pull the English out. While that was in progress, the Dutch and English were coexisting on one of the last English settlements, the island of Ambon. This small piece of volcanic land, 30 miles long by ten miles wide, saw coexistence between these two European powers as difficult at best. Both nations were operating under a treaty wherein they were obliged to work with each other. However, the British did not cooperate with the Dutch on either financial or military commitments made under a 1619 treaty between the two nations. The Dutch governor, Herman van Speult, had dealt with a few insurrections and mutinies and was understandably suspicious. However, by 1623 it was general knowledge that the English were about to pull out. But van Speult, without warning and for reasons unknown, arrested fourteen Englishmen and ten Japanese mercenaries, accusing them of plotting to take over the main fort on the island. The Japanese were executed and, shortly thereafter, ten of the English as well, but not before being tortured in the fort's dungeons until they confessed. Finally, they were convicted and beheaded. There was no evidence that the men were plotting to seize the fort, which would have been a daunting, if not impossible, task. The Dutch recalled van Speult,

Harvesting cloves in the spice islands in the 17th century. The clove tree is an evergreen with thin and smooth bark. It grows to a height of 9–12 metres (30–40 feet) with a straight trunk.

but he died before he could return home. The British were outraged, and this heinous act convinced them that they needed to give up the Spice Islands. The 'Ambon Massacre', as it came to be called, remained a strong force in the animosity the British felt toward the Dutch. Later, this negative feeling played out when Oliver Cromwell went to war with the Dutch in the 1650s and Charles II did the same over a decade later.

The spice trade and the competition that was ever present in battles and wars between the competing nations took its toll on lives and psyches. John Keay in *The Spice Route* points out that the Reverend Samuel Purchas wrote that the mayhem in the Moluccas could best be attributed 'to the pernicious abandon induced by equatorial temperatures; decent men, Dutch and English, shed their "solid virtues" with their thick European clothes, became excited by the "fiery ferity" of their own spices, and surrendered themselves to the "heathenish qualities of their swarthy associates".'

There was one shining success in the British experience in the Moluccas, but it did not actually occur there. In 1665, the year before this occurrence, the English captured two richly laden Dutch ships and docked in Erith in Kent. The writer Samuel Pepys, recently appointed the Surveyor-Victualer to the Royal Navy, hearing of the cargo, went to the ships and marvelled:

> The greatest wealth lie in confusion that a man can see in the world. Pepper scattered through every chink, you trod upon it; and in cloves and nutmegs I walked above the knees; whole rooms full. And silk in bales, and boxes of copper plate, one of which I saw opened . . . as noble a sight as ever I saw in my life.

Pepys also concluded some business on the side, according to the historian Simon Schama in his 1997 book *The Embarrassment of Riches*. The famed diarist was found in the taverns of the port buying up spices from 'dirty wretched seamen' in verminous taverns. Additionally, the gossip was that men in high places had helped themselves to riches that belonged in the royal treasury. These 'riches' acquired by Pepys and others, dazzled by such affluence, were of minor

Painted map of Ambonia in the East Indies with a portrait of its first
Dutch Governor, Frederik Houtman. Ambonia was the scene of the 1623
massacre of Englishmen, Japanese and a Portuguese by the Dutch that
ended any hope of Anglo–Dutch co-operation in spice trading.

concern to the Dutch, who had been acquiring many more
spice-laden ships from the east. The majority of the spice
wealth was docked in Amsterdam.

The year 1665 saw the occurrence of a significant real
estate exchange. A historical fact that many people are aware
of is that in 1626 the Dutch bought the island of Manhattan
from the Canarsee Indians for a few trinkets. What is less
known about this two-part transaction, however, is the way
in which the English acquired it from the Dutch soon afterwards. The fascinating story is centred on spices. Around
1616 the Dutch East India Company was able to secure a
source of nutmeg by occupying Pulo Run, a small volcanic
island in the Banda Islands, west of New Guinea. The nutmeg crop here was small, but the British had one outpost
among the Dutch-controlled Spice Islands. In March 1665
two English ships pulled into Pulo Run, taking it over and
forcing the Dutch to leave. However, a short time after the
incident, the Dutch returned in greater numbers and ousted

the English, destroying the island's entire nutmeg crop, with the result that no one could profit from it. Meanwhile, the British decided to retaliate, not in the East Indies, but in New Amsterdam. When an English fleet came into the Hudson River at Fort Amsterdam, they found a Dutch garrison that had overestimated both the firepower of the British fleet and the number of fighting men facing their settlement. There were four ships in all, and only one of them a man-of-war, the others being simple trading vessels. The Dutch leader Peter Stuyvesant had been told there were 800 men but, in reality, there was less than half that number aboard the four ships. The Dutch gave in, and the English took over, naming the area New York. Later, in the Treaty of Breda, the Dutch retained the island of Run and the British held on to New York. This exchange of a small nutmeg-growing island for Manhattan turned out to be a major historical event. It also represented a dramatic shift of global power, as the British concentrated their Asian efforts on India and moved their western focus to North America and the Caribbean.

Cross-cultural Convergence

Unrelenting heat was an aspect of the tropics that made life uncomfortable for spice seekers. Compounding this was a lack of knowledge about the people native to these spice-rich lands. Cross-cultural living of any kind was not an easy task in the days of spice trading and the settlements that grew up to support them. Giles Milton in *Nathaniel's Nutmeg* reports that 'the annals of the East India Company are filled with notices of plagues, sicknesses and deaths that occurred in Bantam'. The journal of the seventeenth-century English sinologist Edmund Scott depicts the horrors of life in this disease-ridden port. Scott watched his two superiors die and numerous sailors succumb to typhoid and cholera. Malaria was rife in these tidal swamplands situated by the Sunda Strait. To add to this misery were the confusion and misperceptions caused by the cultural mixing of Chinese, Indians, Christians and Muslims, all living yards apart. And on top of this, the indigenous Javanese people despised them all, tolerating them only for the benefit of trade. Moreover, in times of tension and armed conflict, the Javanese could not distinguish between the Dutch and English, a constant challenge to native alliances formed with either of these powers. Finally, as Milton reports, there were roving bands of headhunters who were constantly in need of 'products'. Daily life in the spice trade, and the 'cultural encounters' that ensued were indeed daunting, unpredictable adventures. In his 2006 book, *Pathfinders*, Felipe Fernández-Armesto, the global historian, evocatively sums up the experience of Europeans in the tropics: 'They began with embraces, continued with abuse, and ended in bloodshed.'

The Role of the Chinese

The question as to where the Chinese were in this long chapter of the spice trade story can be said to have two short responses: that they were already there or that they had come and gone. In the centuries before the Europeans came to Asia, the Chinese were engaged in trading networks that brought them pepper, cloves, nutmeg and cinnamon. Trade in Asia was so interactive that the Chinese did not have to exert much effort to get the spices they wanted. However, in the fifteenth century, they launched a global expedition that may very well have been greater than any the world has ever seen. Early in the 1400s, before the Portuguese arrived in Asia, the Chinese sent seven expeditions to the West under the leadership of Admiral Zheng He. The first of these voyages comprised sixty-two junks, 225 support vessels and over 27,000 men. Zheng He's junk was a technological marvel. Some accounts have its length at more than 130 metres (142 yards) and width at 60 metres (65 yards). It had nine masts running fore to aft. (The ship was as long as 1½ American football fields and bigger than a 60 by 100-yard football/ soccer pitch.) In comparison, a Portuguese caravel that sailed to India was under 100 feet long. Zheng He may have led the greatest sea armada in history. Another question is: if the Chinese already had access to spices, what was the purpose of these voyages? It is generally agreed that these were flag-waving expeditions meant to demonstrate the power and might of the Ming Dynasty. Moreover, the Chinese were also interested in documenting all the ports visited and products encountered by the voyages, and maps and sailing records were known to have been returned to China. The seven expeditions visited about 32 countries all over the Indian Ocean, west to Africa and east to the Spice Islands. Zheng He even presented a giraffe from Africa to the emperor, a singular and exciting event in the Chinese court. During his septet of trips abroad, the admiral also brought back lions, camels, ostriches, zebras, rhinoceroses and other African wildlife.

All this seafaring by the Chinese could have meant domination over the Indian Ocean traffic in spices and other goods. However, history played a hand in the form of court intrigue: Zheng's successes created problems for the imperial court, whose power was shifting to a more Confucian philosophical system that honoured values such as taking care of the home front and dealing with outsiders and barbarians only as the need arose. This sea change of thinking halted future ocean-bound movement for China (and, sadly, even resulted in the records of Zheng He being destroyed). Consider what the consequences for Portugal and other European nations would have been if China had continued its seafaring empire into the sixteenth century. Despite curtailing its ocean-going ways, from the end of these voyages forward, the Chinese and their spice-trading empire of coastal shipping and commerce continued as the dominant force in Asian economics. This period of history in the East did not see any expansion of empires. South Asia had trading networks and fleets but was not assertive toward others. In Japan the warlords were dividing up the country, the empires of Java were in the past, and the Thai and Burmese efforts at imperialism were yet to come. Trade flourished, and the Europeans, despite local conflicts, took their share of spices without interference.

The French and Danes Play a Part

During the seventeenth and eighteenth centuries, France and Denmark played small roles in the spice trade. Both nations based their operations not on the Malabar coast of India or in the Spice Islands but on the south-east coast of India, the base for textiles and cloth that were desired all over Asia and Africa. Here they joined the Dutch and the English, who also realized the great value of the Indian cloth that supplied many global markets and afforded access to East Asian spices.

The French had attempted to enter the spice trade more directly at the beginning of the sixteenth century. Initially, and with the unofficial support of the king, freebooters started pirating Portuguese ships that were carrying Asian spices to

A lady bringing spices to a lawyer in France in the time of Louis XIV, no doubt in payment of a fee.

the north of Europe from Lisbon to Antwerp. Additionally, French vessels from various western ports intercepted Portuguese ships returning from India off the west coast of Africa or in other parts of the Atlantic. The French also established royal ports for the importation of spices into France. Over time they became carriers of the spices for Venetian or Genoese traders, and eventually Marseilles became a major centre for spices. The French made one venture into Asia from the port of Dieppe after 1527. Two ships set out for the Moluccas, running a Portuguese blockade and making it to Sumatra. Two of the leaders died of fever after failing to deal with Sumatran leaders or trade for spices. One of the vessels returned home in 1530, convincing the French to leave the spice trade to the Portuguese. However, French piracy of Iberian vessels continued along the Atlantic coast.

The French had established a colony in 1693 on the southern Coromandel coast of India at Pondicherry (now Puducherry). They later built a factory on the west coast north of Calicut. It was in India that the French traded cloth for spices and other products such as rice, timber, rope and cowries (shells used as currency in the Indian Ocean world). In the 1770s, the East Indian monopoly on spices was broken when the French governor of Mauritius smuggled out clove and nutmeg seedlings to the island he oversaw. From here, the clove was taken to Zanzibar by the Arab trader, Harameli bin Saleh, in 1818. In time Zanzibar and Pemba, on the East African coast, became two of the largest suppliers of cloves to the world markets.

Changes in Gallic cuisine and the use of spices in French cooking had a direct effect on the French world of spice trading. Prior to the mid-seventeenth century, the French employed various spices in food preparation. However, after the publication of *Le cuisinier françois* in 1651 by the chef François La Varenne, the French shifted away from the use of spices and instead concentrated on dishes where the ingredients were cooked in their own juices or made with butter and other home-made or home-grown products.

Thus, over time the French purchased and consumed fewer spices in the preparation of authentically French cuisine. One of the ironies of this transition away from spices was the opulence of the court of Louis XIV where baskets of spices were brought before the king prior to a royal feast. However, this was the end of an era climaxing with the French Revolution. Spices still play a minor role in traditional French cooking – in dishes such as Béarnaise sauce which uses white peppercorns, cayenne pepper and tarragon leaves over Beef Tournedos. Often a little black pepper is added at the end. The French also use nutmeg in preparing filet of sole with spinach and Bechamel (or Mornay) sauce.

The Danes began their exploits into Asia in the seventeenth century, sending out ships to bring back pepper and cloves. However, this trade was limited to only seven ships returning to the homeland with spices between 1622 and 1637. Decades later, Denmark established an East India company of its own, but Dutch dominance forced them west from the Spice Islands to the east coast of India, where they also developed a textile base for trade in Asia. It was not until the eighteenth century that the Danes opened trade with China and, as a result, other Asian ports. The Danish East India Company did especially well during the time when Holland and France were at war with England and spices needed to be moved back to Europe by a neutral carrier.

Eastern Spices Move West

While Central and South America were to be the source of one of the great world spices that emigrated to the East, North America, during the period of English colonization in the early seventeenth century, found spices in its settlers' diet as a result of global trade. One of these colonies, Maryland, founded at St Mary's in 1634, is known to have used spices in its diet. In *Narratives of Early Maryland* organizers recommended spices as one of the staples that a colonist would need to settle in for one year. Inventories of deceased members of colonial Maryland families listed spices as part of their estates. In the 1650s, for example, a John Ward listed a pound of pepper as well as ginger, nutmeg and mace among those items inventoried. A decade later, in the much larger estate of Robert Coles, pepper, saffron, nutmeg, cloves and cinnamon were listed. The source of some of these spices might have been Dutch ships that were trading at St Mary's frequently during the 1640s, when the English were distracted by their civil war.

Chilli Peppers Move Westwards to Dominate the East

So far most of the emphasis of this world history of spices has been on the Indian Ocean area and the Spice Islands. The story now shifts to the western hemisphere, where the capsicum vegetable enters the spice story. The tropical plant known as the capsicum (from the Latin word *capsa*, meaning 'case' or 'box') is native to the Americas and belongs to the same family as the tomato and aubergine. There are basically two main categories of capsicum – sweet peppers and chilli (chili or chile) peppers – and from these hundreds of variations are grown all over the world. Amazingly, chilli peppers did not originally exist anywhere in Europe or in Asia. Indeed today it is hard to imagine China, Thailand, Korea and other Asian and African nations without this ubiquitous spice. How it moved around the

Chillies laid out to dry in Ethiopia. The chilli has travelled more widely than any other spice and been used in dishes from different cultures.

world through trade and cuisine is a complex and still ongoing history.

The earliest known evidence of chilli peppers is found at pre-Columbian sites in Peru. When the Spanish arrived in Mexico in the early sixteenth century, Hernán Cortés described the Aztecs growing and eating peppers. The conquistador and his men also had the fiery experience (and honour) of being offered a chocolate drink laced with hot peppers – although they were also presented with a less fiery alternative sweetened with cane sugar.

The chilli was part of the native diet of Central and South America, and there are hundreds of varieties of it. This pepper is so old that it is difficult to trace the origin of the plant to one or more sources. Evidence of its growth goes back to 7000 BCE, while farming of it dates to roughly 5000 BCE. The chilli was grown by the Toltecs, Mayas and Aztecs in Central America and by the Incas to the south. The latter three used them in their torture rituals, and they were also used as a 'poison' for arrow tips. Fish were also deliberately killed with chilli 'poison' that was dropped in the water.

Christopher Columbus brought the chilli pepper back to Spain. However, the Italian explorer was only interested in black pepper, cinnamon, cloves and nutmeg and less concerned with native plants unless he thought they might be related to these four premium spices. Nonetheless, the doctor on his voyage, Alvarez Chanca, from Seville, identified the spice and took it back to Spain, where it was used only sparingly in foods and was found to have more applications in medicine. In her 1987 book, *History of Food*, Maguelonne Toussaint-Samat writes that the chilli pepper was considered a panacea for intestinal infections, parasites and diarrhoea . . . and even a remedy for piles. Although the capsicum did not play a strong role in Spanish cuisine, there is some evidence of its use as food in Iberia. An annual festival in Galicia, in north-western Spain on the Bay of Biscay, is held to celebrate a small green chilli pepper that is fried. The Basques of northern Spain also used the peppers in their chorizo sausages and in dishes with tomatoes and cod.

The early global migration of the chilli pepper could be due to the Portuguese, who were establishing their colonies in Asia just after the chilli arrived on the Iberian peninsula. Brazil was also a site of peppers in the Americas for the Portuguese. How much the Portuguese were influenced by the pepper brought back by the Spanish is not known. What is more likely is that the Portuguese found and promoted the chilli of southern Brazil, taking it around the world to their Asian bases, including the ports in Macao and Goa. From there they came to influence Chinese and Indian food. One sixteenth-century botanist referred to chilli pepper from Goa on the west coast of India as 'Pernambuco peppers', a direct reference to an area of Brazil. The chilli also found its

Capsicum annuum. Chilli has become a dominant world spice, moving from west to east and around the world.

way into Africa, when the Portuguese conducted their notorious slave trading on that continent. Slaves brought to Brazil for the plantations continued these traditions, while the chilli continued to evolve into new variations as it was replanted in newly developed lands.

In Central America, the Aztec and evolving Mexican diets were based on maize (corn), beans, tomatoes and capsicum peppers. At the time of Columbus, the peppers were eaten in soups and stews as well as with fish and meat. They were also dried and made into a variety of pickles to take on journeys. As the Spanish moved north and west throughout the Americas, the chilli pepper moved into California with the Jesuit priests, who established new missions at least 400 miles north into the present-day state of California. Today, much of the chilli powder in the United States comes from that state.

A legend that makes for good fiction tells how the chilli pepper evolved into paprika, the national spice of Hungary. In the seventeenth century, the Ottoman Empire controlled much of Eastern Europe, including Budapest. The story goes that a Turkish pasha named Mehmet saw a beautiful Hungarian water-girl and quickly put her in his harem. Confined to the pasha's gardens, she became familiar with all types of plants. One of these was a vine that bore large red fruit, which the Turks ground into a powder to spice up their food. The water-girl had never tasted anything as good, so secretly she gathered up some seeds. It happened that the girl had been in love with a peasant boy before her abduction. While she was in the harem, she discovered a secret passage that the pasha had dug as a means of escape in times of trouble. Each night she went through the passage and met her lover. On one occasion she gave him some of the seeds, which he then planted. After a year, paprika plants were growing all over Budapest and its countryside, and the

Hungarians embraced the new spice. Later, there was a revolution in which the Turks were driven out of Hungary, but paprika nonetheless grew to become the nation's chief spice.

The paprika most Westerners enjoy today is very flavourful but mild. However, in Hungary more than two dozen variations of the spice have been developed, and they have varying degrees of heat. The Hungarians more or less adopted it as their national spice when it was made a central ingredient in goulash, the spicy stew that is the country's best-known traditional dish. Mild paprika is made from the seeds of the pepper, while hotter varieties come from the whole spice pod, which is dried and then ground.

The real migration of the chilli pepper in Eastern Europe was first into Greece, then into the northern Balkan countries, and then eastwards to Turkey. Eventually it migrated into southern Italy. The pepper did not make inroads into the north of Europe at this time, however, largely for botanical and climatic reasons (Hungary was considered the northern limit of chilli pepper growth). The name 'paprika' came from the Greek term for black pepper, *peperi*. Other name changes occurred as the spice moved through regional languages such as Greek, in which it is called *piperia*. More than anything else, the chilli pepper was born to travel. All that was needed was the seed and the transplanting and, in many areas of the world, such as India, where the climate was right, the process was quite effortless.

Spices Migrate to the West

Once spices became more available to a larger portion of the population in Europe, they assumed a larger role in both medicine and in food preparation. In fact, it is generally believed that at first spices were primarily used in medicine, only later taking their rightful place in the kitchen. In his *Regimen corpus* (1256), Aldobrandino of Siena wrote that cinnamon was good for 'fortifying the liver and the stomach' and 'cooking meat thoroughly . . . ' while cloves 'fortify the stomach and body . . . eliminate flatulence and evil humours . . . due to cold, and help to cook food thoroughly'.

According to *Le Trésor de santé*, written by a celebrated French doctor and published in Lyon in 1607, pepper 'maintains health, fortifies the stomach . . . (and) eliminates winds. It facilitates urination . . . cures chills from intermittent fevers, and also heals snakebites and hastens the expulsion of stillborn infants from the womb. If drunk [it] is good for coughs . . . Ground up with dried grapes, [it] purges the brain of phlegm and stimulates the appetite.' Cloves were good 'for the eyes, liver, heart and stomach'. Oil of clove was 'excellent for treating toothaches. It is good for stomach fluxions due to cold and for cold maladies of the stomach.' However, as this ditty from a fifteenth-century *Commonplace Book* shows, spices such as pepper were becoming an integral part of the European diet:

Snow is white and lieth in the dike,
And everyman lets it lie;
Pepper is black and has a good smack,
And every man doth it buy.

When all is said and done about the history of spices, there has always been much – and deserved – ado about the Age of Exploration and the roles played by the Portuguese, Dutch, Spanish, English, Danish and French. Historically, it was an exciting time, an age of converging cultures with all of their challenges. These nations did take the initiative of

Pepper vines growing in Mexico during the 1930s. Pepper spread out from India to other tropical areas after the 16th century. Today Vietnam is the world's largest producer.

connecting West and East, and they did change their economies with the influx of spices and other Eastern goods. A significant fact about the spice trade is that these products became more reasonably priced after Vasco da Gama returned. The main reason for this is that using a direct sea route from Asia to Europe, as opposed to the overland route across Arabia to the Mediterranean, eliminated many middlemen. Fewer hands in the spice pot meant less expense at the end. But, during this age, and for at least a century afterwards, Europeans gained only a small percentage of the total spice trade. The Middle Eastern and South and East Asian economies flourished, as they did before the Europeans came, consuming most of the world's spices. Trading networks, such as those across the Muslim world, were conducted in an effortless way and 'sealed with a hand-shake and a glance at heaven'. It was, however, the first global age and, as a result of this West–East convergence, the known world expanded beyond belief and was never the same again.

4
The Age of Industrialization

I speak severely to my boy,
I beat him when he sneezes;
For he can thoroughly enjoy
The pepper when he pleases.
Alice's Adventures in Wonderland, Lewis Carroll

As the nineteenth century dawned, the spice trade found a new competitor in the western hemisphere that explored and exploited Sumatra and the Spice Islands. But these traders from the newly founded United States of America faced constant danger in north-west Sumatra from the creese, a short wavy-bladed dagger of the native Malays. France pulled off a coup in the spice world by stealing a spice plant from the Moluccas and successfully transplanting it on the other side of the Indian Ocean. This move led to new growth sites of this spice and to an eventual domination in world sales. However, it also led to a slave system in East Africa that took over a century to erase. The British were to control the Dutch spice empire for a short time during the Napoleonic Wars, but they gave that up, moving on to dominate the South Asian subcontinent and, in the process, changing the spice-consuming habits of their mother

Dutch spice trader in the East Indies. The Dutch continued to deal with local villages in the Spice Islands well into the 20th century.

country. The Dutch regained their spice island world and settled into an orderly and well-controlled system of spice trading.

The British Expand Their Spice World

When Britain took over Holland's colonies in the Indies, the occupation was organized from Malacca by the governor-general of India, Lord Minto, with the help of Thomas Stamford Raffles, later the developer of Singapore. The British introduced many reforms to improve the lives of the people who cared for and produced the spices during the Napoleonic Wars. Raffles's newly instituted land-tax system worked so well that the Dutch retained it when they took back their possessions after the defeat of Napoleon in 1816. It was during this time of British possession that spice seedlings were taken to India and Europe and transplanted successfully.

Edward Coles, an official of the British East India Company, had successfully transplanted nutmeg and clove seedlings on the south-western coast of Sumatra, and black pepper was successfully grown in Penang, an island off the west coast of the Malay Peninsula. Raffles eventually took over these plantations for the East India Company, building a home there which he called the 'Abode of Peace'. His driveway was lined with clove trees, which his second wife, Sophia, described thus: 'The spicy fragrance with which they perfume the air, produce, in driving through a long line of them, a degree of exquisite pleasure.' Britain's short control of the Dutch spice areas had expanded their spice empire, and the British colony of Singapore became a centre of the spice trade. As a result, spices prospered during England's domain, and the prices on the world spice markets were kept at a reasonable level.

Over time Singapore became a human blending of the overland Chinese (the majority), South Asian Indians and

Cutting and quilling cinnamon: cinnamon is cut after heavy rains when the sap is active and the bark can be detached more easily. The best grade is nearly as thin as paper.

Malays. Also influenced by nearby Indonesia and the spice islands, this small nation at the southern tip of the Malay Peninsula was a cross-cultural centre for South East Asia. Their foods and spices reflected this cross-cultural blending. One type of curry that has evolved in Singapore is a blend used to cover seafood before cooking. It consists of coriander, cumin, red chillis from India, fennel, cassia, cardamom, turmeric and tellicherry (Malabar coast of India) black pepper. Today Singapore offers a Spice Garden Tour followed by cooking classes where you can learn to make spice paste.

In the 1850s one of the great British scientists of the nineteenth century was spending years in the Malay Archipelago studying the region's flora and fauna. Alfred Russel Wallace, the man who developed the theory of evolution before Charles Darwin, was busy at work in the land of Eastern spices. As Wallace travelled through the many islands of present-day Indonesia and Malaysia, he outlined the transition of power in the world of nutmeg, mace and cloves. He spoke of the native sultans, Muslim sovereigns who had controlled the spice trade, then came to be dominated by the Portuguese, and later found themselves under Dutch control. The Dutch imposed their will on the local leaders and very strictly regulated the growth of cloves and nutmeg in order to control the prices on world markets. For the sultans, Wallace wrote, the Dutch system meant a regular supply of income from spices, replacing an earlier spice world that featured Portuguese domination and fluctuating prices for both nutmeg and cloves. Additionally, under the Dutch, the sultans had regained political control of their people, something that had been lost under the Portuguese.

In his classic book, *The Malay Archipelago*, Wallace offered fine descriptions of the plant and animal life of these islands. Here, he describes the nutmeg:

Leadenhall Street, a 19th-century watercolour by Thomas Halton. This was the London street where the British East India Company was located.

Few cultivated plants are more beautiful than nutmeg-trees. They are handsomely shaped and glossy-leaved, growing to the height of twenty to thirty feet, and bearing small yellowish flowers. The fruit is the size and color of a peach, but rather oval. It is of a tough fleshy consistence, but when ripe splits open, and shows the dark brown nut within, covered with the crimson mace, and is then a most beautiful object. Within the thin hard shell of the nut is the seed, which is the nutmeg of commerce. The nuts are eaten by the large pigeons of Banda, which digest the mace but cast up the nut with its seed uninjured.

Loading Muntok pepper (early 20th century). Muntok is a seaport on the western side of Bangka Island, located off the south-east coast of Sumatra. It is noted for its white pepper, which is formed after the green berries are picked and soaked and then left to dry in the sun.

The British centre for the spice trade was, appropriately, on Mincing Lane in London. This thoroughfare, stretching from Fenchurch Street south to Great Tower Street, was for some years the world's leading centre for spices as well as for tea. In 1799, after the British East India Company took over all the trading ports of the Dutch East India Company, Mincing Lane became a dominant centre for the global spice trade. With the demise of the British East India Company in 1834, the lane was used as a centre for tea company offices. As the England of the nineteenth century was gradually influenced by Indian dishes, one domestic product underwent a transformation in the upper classes. In London the working classes were eating their eels, and later their chips, in plain vinegar while the upper classes were developing an appetite for tart, chilli-flavoured sauces. In 1845 Eliza Acton, in her *Modern Cookery for Private Families*, recommended the use of chilli vinegar as an addition to tomato sauce. Moreover, her tomato ketchup recipe included three dozen capsicum chilli peppers for every gallon or half peck of tomatoes. The chilli pepper migrated east to India and was now playing a culinary role in Great Britain.

The French Transplant Cloves

Nations that controlled islands where spices were grown were extremely protective of their crops. The Dutch, above all, were highly sensitive about protection. To stop their nutmeg from being reseeded, they covered this export crop with lime. The Dutch also set their clove groves on fire both to control the market and to keep others from getting a new crop from the plants. During the Age of Exploration and into the nineteenth century, there were many attempts by European nations to steal spice seeds or plants. In the last quarter of the eighteenth century, a French adventurer, Pierre Poivre (Peter Pepper) was successful. Poivre had spent a great deal of time in Asia as a young man, doing various types of work for the French. At different times he was a prisoner of the Dutch, and he lost an arm when his ship was taken by the British near the Straits of Malacca. He was especially interested in botany and decided to try to bring tropical plants into French hands. On a few occasions he attempted to transplant clove and nutmeg onto French soil, but the seedlings always died. He eventually settled on Mauritius, in the south-west Indian Ocean just east of Madagascar. Working there as a French political official, he built a house and started a garden of tropical plants on the island. He soon returned to the Moluccas in search of spices and was lucky to run across a disenchanted Dutchman who directed him to an island where he could obtain a preponderance of nutmeg and clove seedlings from natives who were secretly growing

Clove tree. Cloves originated on five small islands in the East Indies. The clove tree grows better on small islands but away from the sea.

and hiding them from the Dutch. So the aptly named Frenchman was able to bring a large quantity of seedlings back to Mauritius to his garden. The die had been cast, and Poivre's determination and dual interest in botany and serving France had allowed for the beginning of a new clove empire (a fellow countryman considered Poivre's coup comparable to the stealing of the Golden Fleece by Jason). By the last decade of the eighteenth century, the clove had been successfully transplanted to Madagascar and then to Zanzibar and Pemba, which today rank as the three largest clove producers in the world. Cloves were also moved into the Caribbean on St Kitts by the English, who had most likely stolen them from the French West Indies. In 1818, of the 78,000 pounds of cloves sold in England, 70,000 came from St Kitts. The nutmeg was transplanted to the Caribbean at Martinique and on the island of Grenada, which later became the world's largest producer of nutmeg. It should be noted that the Portuguese, who had earlier lost their spice empire to the Dutch, attempted to grow cloves, nutmeg, cinnamon and pepper in their vast colony of Brazil. The adaptation of spices was successful in many cases if the latitude and botanical conditions allowed for it to happen.

Cloves and Slavery

Trade between Africa and the Arab world had existed for centuries. There were trade connections between Africa, India and Asia involving slaves, gold and ivory. The original inhabitants of Zanzibar were Hadimu, Tumbatu and Pemba peoples, who had been drawn out from interior Africa by the fresh water and fertile soil of the large island off East Africa. In the late tenth century, Persians came to the island, settled there briefly, and then left to be replaced by Arabs from Oman. Zanzibar became a focal point for commerce, since it served as an entry point in East Africa for trade links with the interior. Prior to Portuguese exploration of the East African coast, many Indians from South Asia migrated to Zanzibar where they served as shopkeepers, traders and skilled workers. The Portuguese briefly ruled Zanzibar until 1550, when they were ousted by the Sultan of Oman. For a few centuries Zanzibar was a corner of a global trade network where Africans, Arabs, Chinese, Europeans, Indians and Persians met. In the 1830s a new sultan had moved the Oman capital from Muscat to Zanzibar, setting up clove plantations on Zanzibar and Pemba. This Muslim leader, Seyed Saia, forced most of the Hadimu people to work on the plantations, moving them to the eastern part of the island. Zanzibar then became the world's biggest producer of cloves as well as the largest slave-trading centre on the East African coast. The trade in cloves and slaves was mostly financed by the Indian merchants working for Bombay (present-day Mumbai) firms. The cloves were shipped to other parts of Africa, to India and to Persia. The French clove plantations on Mauritius thrived due to the shipment of slaves from the Great Slave Market in Zanzibar. French slave traders were very influential in the spread of the clove trade. The English explorer Richard Burton attributed the development of clove oil, a favourite of the Zanzibar peoples, to M. Sausse, a Creole from the Mascarenes, a series of islands east of Madagascar, where Mauritius and Reunion lie.

The British became involved with Zanzibar in the late eighteenth century and throughout the nineteenth century. The public in Great Britain increased its interest in Zanzibar because the explorers Burton, David Livingstone and John Speke launched their expeditions there. The British signed treaties with the sultan to protect Zanzibar in exchange for

Spice box from a waterfront museum in St John's, New Brunswick, Canada.

Omani support against the French. Britain had outlawed slavery in 1807 and made many attempts to influence the Sultan of Zanzibar to do the same. Agreements were signed to eliminate slavery in the 1870s, but progress was slow. Zanzibar was an increasingly important trading centre, and from the 1820s onwards, American, German and British trading ships had established Zanzibar as a major port.

The Impact of the United States on the Spice Trade

Meanwhile, in the first decade of its existence as a nation, the United States was starting to make an impact on the global pepper trade. The country's involvement began in a small port north west of Boston, Massachusetts, called Salem. Here an enterprising sea captain named Jonathan Carnes set out on a voyage to the East Indies in 1793, with no intent other than to explore possible areas of trade. While in Sumatra, Carnes learned of pepper. He was able to acquire a small amount of the spice but did not visit the ports where larger quantities were available. On his return home, his ship was wrecked off the coast of Bermuda, but he eventually reached Salem, all the while keeping his knowledge of the pepper ports secret. He secured financial backing and built a large ship. In 1795 he set sail on the 130-ton *Rajah*, with four guns, a ten-man crew and a secret destination. The cargo consisted of two pipes (a pipe is equivalent to four barrels) of brandy, 58 cases of gin and 12 tons of iron, along with tobacco, salmon and other items. Eighteen months later, the ship returned with a bulk of pepper that reaped a profit of 700 per cent.

Others in Salem were curious, but they were not able to determine where Carnes had gone. A few set out for

Salem, Massachusetts' city seal. Influenced by Salem's dominant black pepper trade in the early 19th century, the seal depicts an oriental person, ship and the Latin motto 'To the farthest port of the rich East.'

Bencoolen (Bengkulu, the present-day capital of Indonesia's Bengkulu province), and it was not until 1801 and 1802 that the ship *America*, under the respective commands of Captain John Crowninshield and Captain Jeremiah Briggs, brought to Salem 815,792 pounds of pepper and the next year 760,000 pounds of the spice. The aggregate duty paid on these two cargoes was $103,874.03. Salem was to be the pepper port of note, on both sides of the Atlantic, for the first half of the nineteenth century. Except during the war of 1812, when ports were blockaded by the British, Salem supplied not only the eastern United States but also much of Europe with black pepper. It is an interesting point of history that at the beginning of this trade the residents of the eastern United States were not familiar with black pepper as part of their diet. With this in mind, the Salem merchants and their seamen who flourished in the pepper trade were not so much thinking of supplying the North American market but, rather, delivering the pepper to Europe to exchange for other products with a high value at home, such as French wine. For over three-quarters of a century after the onset of this trade, almost a thousand voyages were made between Salem and Sumatra in the East Indies. When these early eastward-bound expeditions set out from Salem to venture around the Cape of Good Hope, the geography skills of the seafarers were rough and untested. Early voyages in search of pepper could have meant India or further east. Each Salem sea captain had to learn his own way. As it turned out, the eventual destination and focus of the pepper trade centred on Sumatra.

The adventures of these 'down East' mariners in the East Indies is the stuff of novels and movies. Narratives from accounts such as *Salem Vessels and Their Voyages* and *Pepper and Pirates* relate many tales of these New England sailors encountering new cultures and navigating unknown waters around the island of Sumatra. This large island was typical of many of those making up the Indonesian Archipelago, tropical in nature, many with active volcanoes, and all linked to the seas.

The people of north and north-west Sumatra were the Achnese, who historically had controlled the trade passing through the Straits of Malacca to the east. They were Muslim traders and warriors, and their capital was Banda Aceh at the northern tip of the island nation. The Dutch were to discover how difficult it would be to control the Achnese as they established their spice empire in the East

Indies later in the nineteenth century. An affront to one Achnese might be an insult to all. Different trading centres were controlled by rajahs, each with its own history of trade with Europeans and other Asian traders over the centuries. However, one of the first adventures of Captain Carnes and his Salem crew was not with the Achnese. In the *Scents of Eden*, Charles Corn vividly describes an encounter:

> One evening late, Carnes was pacing the small quarter-deck, while the sounds of jungle on a moonlit night filled the bay. He made his way forward, dimly making out the anchor watch alert in the dense darkness before turning aft, passing two seamen of the port watch who murmured a greeting before Carnes returned to his solitary promenade on the quarterdeck.
>
> A half hour passed, then an hour. Carnes considered turning in, but it was close and humid below, and a soft breeze made it pleasant on deck. Suddenly a shout went up from the bow watch. 'Boat ahoy, who's there?' he challenged in the darkness. Carnes, suspecting Malay pirates, had just turned to sound the alarm below when he was rocked by the heavy impact of another boat. Men hurried up the latterway, seizing pikes as they emerged from the hatch to repulse the attackers who were attempting to board.
>
> A figure rose over the rail, and the mate fired, hitting his target, who fell backward, but another replaced the first. The bow watch, with no weapon, tried to push the intruder back, but a cutlass severed his left hand. Other mates came to his aid, and the attackers pushed off.
>
> In the darkness the attackers identified themselves as French, having misidentified the American vessel for a British one.

Men of the *Rajah* stood to arms now under lantern light as Frenchmen came aboard, uttering exclamations of regret, while their lieutenant, who had led the attack, lay dead in the longboat and the maimed sailor was carried below.

Today the term 'global/local' is used to describe how local life is influenced by global events. The last people Carnes expected on his boat were French soldiers and sailors, but the Napoleonic wars, fought mostly in Europe and North Africa, reached these American traders near the Straits of Malacca in the late 1790s.

Two days before Thanksgiving in November 1805, the ship *Putnam*, from Salem, commanded by Captain John Carlton, was captured by the Malays and several of the crew were massacred. The captain had finished his trading, and two British ships were anchored nearby. While Carlton was gone, the crew of a Malay boat had been allowed to board the *Putnam* and wander about the ship at will. When Captain Carlton returned, he found an alarmed crew fearful of the Malays. Carlton sent a small crew out from the ship to warn the Malays not to return. Later that day a Malay boat approached the *Putnam*, and the captain ordered the crew to be on deck and ready for an attack. However, the visitors were Chinese merchants who wanted to trade with the officers and crew. The Malays remained in their boat.

On Thanksgiving Day, the captain had one more settlement to make with the traders on shore, and as he left he noted a Malay brig well off to his south. There was a strong north wind, which Carlton felt would keep the Malays away. However, during his absence on shore, the wind dropped, and a Malay crew of sixteen men approached his ship, claiming they had pepper they wanted to pass on board. Six

Malays were allowed to bring the pepper up, and they did not appear to be armed with creeses. During the weighing of the pepper, one of the crew members, Samuel Pearson, noticed that two Malays at the ship's rail were being handed creeses from their boat. These curved or wavy Malayan daggers with double-edged blades were something to be feared because they were very effective for hand-to-hand fighting. Pearson gave a cry of alarm and that seemed to be the signal for the Malays to attack. Pearson was stabbed, and now other Malays were climbing aboard the *Putnam*. Several crew members were killed, while others fled over the bow or below. One grabbed a handspike and dispatched two or three Malays before he was stabbed in the back. The ship's carpenter, William Brown, the only crew member left, grabbed a stout stick about four feet long and bolted a coffee grinder to its end to flail away at the attackers. He was stabbed several times but kept fighting. Finally, some other crew members appeared on the scene and, working together, were able to drive the Malays off the ship. On Thanksgiving night it appeared that three members of the crew were dead, two more soon died of their wounds, and two or three more had been badly wounded. One of the British ships took the crew east to Penang on the Malay Peninsula. Eventually, in February 1806, William Brown, the hero of the encounter, arrived in Calcutta, where his account of the incident reached Salem and was printed in the *Salem Gazette* of 4 July 1806.

The Adulteration of Spices

By the nineteenth century the early medieval ideas of spices flowing on rivers from the Garden of Eden had long since faded. When pepper arrived in England in the fourteenth

The Cinnamon Gardens near Columbo

Slaves harvesting cinnamon near Colombo, Sri Lanka (formally Ceylon).

century and was handled by the Guild of Pepperers, higher standards were established for the importation of spices. The guild forbade the soaking of cloves to increase their weight and thus add to their value. They also cracked down on dirt, filth and other waste added to spice containers. The Guild even established the right to enter places of business and seize inferior spices. Adulteration had evolved into many forms such as the reusing of ginger, mixing the old, discarded pieces with the new.

There were also some substances used in adulteration that were harmful to health. In the 1850s a Dr Arthur Hassall compiled a list of thirty substances which he had discovered in food and drinks, some of which used deadly poisons. Cayenne pepper contained lead which could induce paralysis. In the 1820s *A Treatise on Adulterations of Food and Culinary*

Poisons exhibiting the Fraudulent Sophistication . . . and Methods of Detecting Them was written by Fredrick Accum. He described the mixture of fake peppercorns with genuine pepper. The fakes were made from the residue of linseed oil extraction mixed with clay and a little cayenne pepper. You could detect the fake by putting all the ingredients in water. The fake would fall apart and the peppercorns would remain whole. Ground pepper was often mixed with dust, dirt or pepper dust to increase the weight.

Cinnamon presents an interesting cross-cultural case of adulteration vis-à-vis the United States and Great Britain. Beginning in the 1820s in England, cinnamon adulteration was claimed when cassia bark was mixed with cinnamon. The British have historically preferred cinnamon to cassia, considering the latter inferior. In the United States cassia is sold as cinnamon, or perhaps, accepted as cinnamon as 'interchangeable in commerce'. Harold McGee in *On Food and Cooking* states that 'most of the cinnamon sold in the United States is actually cassia. The two are most easily distinguished by colour: true cinnamon is tan while cassia is a darker reddish brown.' This is even more confusing when you know that there are three major types of cassia – Chinese, Saigon and Batavia – all with differently coloured bark. One culture's adulterated cinnamon is another culture's cinnamon.

Spices Spread Across the Globe

The nineteenth century witnessed the promulgation of spices all over the world. The Dutch had established a strong control of some of the sovereign spices in the Moluccas, the British had a firm grip on India and its pepper trading and the French had a strong hand in the clove industry, while the

United States supplied South East Asian pepper east and west. Chilli peppers continued to move to East, South East and South Asia, steadily influencing the eating habits of peoples in those regions. Of significant note in this century were the improvements in transportation on both land and sea. The development of steam-powered ships not only made the movement of spices across the globe faster and more efficient, but it also provided a vehicle for people of financial means to travel abroad and experience new cultures and cuisines. The establishment of novel businesses such as Thomas Cook's travel empire allowed both the rich, and the less well off crew members who served them, to become acquainted with new worlds across the globe. On the ground, the development of steam power for trains saw the evolution of extensive railway systems that connected people across land masses and allowed seaborne travellers to move inland. Spices were no longer just an exotic food for the rich – they had become an accessible product for all.

5
The Twentieth Century and Beyond

Pepper love: that's how I think of it.
Abraham and Aurora fell in pepper love,
up there on the Malabar Gold.
The Moor's Last Sigh, Salman Rushdie

In the last century and a half, the spice trade has played a minor role in the British economy. The Dutch, after initially faltering at the end of their period of dominance, made some humanistic reforms in the nineteenth century and, employing a host of progressive scientific agricultural methods, remained at the forefront of the pepper trade until the Second World War. In 1949 Indonesia became independent, and the Dutch had to deal with a new nation and new times, which resulted in their exclusion from exploiting much of their former colony's natural bounty. Taking their place were Chinese overland traders who worked the spice trade.

Also after the Second World War, a boom in spices came about in the United States. American soldiers returning home from the Pacific as well as Europe had experienced new cultures and new tastes, and the spice market grew. Spice consumption in the 1960s and '70s increased at five times the rate of the population growth. By 1990 the United

Market spices on sale in Lanzhou, China.

States accounted for 17 per cent of the world's consumption of spices, with black pepper the primary spice of choice in the country. Today, Vietnam, India, Indonesia and Singapore dominate the global pepper trade.

In this the modern era, where and how spices are grown and treated and how the weather affects them are important issues surrounding their development, sale and distribution. Changing patterns of use are also part of the spice story in the twentieth century and beyond. If you were to ask a historian knowledgeable about the sixteenth- and seventeenth-century spice trade where most of the black pepper in the world is grown today, he or she would most likely say western India, not Vietnam, which in fact leads the world in pepper production in the new millennium. If you were to ask how the nutmeg crops of Grenada in the Caribbean are faring after the devastating Hurricane Ivan wiped out the island's world-dominant crop in 2004, the response would be that nutmeg comes from the Banda Islands in Indonesia, not the Caribbean. Finally, if you were to state that Indonesia is a major importer of cloves needed to support the Kretek clove-cigarette smoking habits of its natives, the historian would be astounded. After all, cloves have their roots in the Spice Islands and for centuries could be found nowhere else. As well, a historian of the early civilizations of the Americas might be dumbfounded to discover that Mexico, the land of the Aztecs, is now importing most of its chilli peppers.

The Rise of McCormick in the Spice Trade

What is today the largest spice company in the world, McCormick, was founded in Baltimore, Maryland, in 1889. The last of the Salem clipper ships came back from Sumatra before the Civil War in the United States. The New England city faded as a port as New York and Boston came to dominate global trade. From this point onwards, and for about a hundred years afterwards, direct contact between the United States and the sources of spices stopped. Amazingly, up until the 1960s, spices for the United States were almost exclusively bought through merchants in New York City, who acted as middlemen in procuring spices from merchants, in countries such as the Netherlands and Germany, where they were in direct contact with spice sources in Asia and Africa. These Europeans arranged for the delivery of spices through the merchants in New York and other global cities historically involved in the spice trade. McCormick, an evolving and growing spice company in the United States, also obtained its products in this manner, even after nearly three-quarters of a century of existence.

By the late 1960s, McCormick began its ascent to the top of the world spice markets by setting up a programme called 'global sourcing'. Hank Kaestner, the now-retired

Bee Brand spice advertisement. From the late nineteenth until the mid-twentieth century McCormick sold its spices under the 'Bee Brand'.

McCormick and Company factory on the Downtown Baltimore Waterfront. From the early to the late 20th century scents of spices filled the air of Baltimore.

global spice buyer for McCormick, began his career at this time, travelling across the world and identifying the best spices at their source. Over the decades until his recent retirement he made some 185 trips to the world's spice-growing areas. Kaestner recounted his feelings about retracing the steps of Vasco da Gama and other explorers of the sixteenth, seventeenth and eighteenth centuries, all of whom were seeking spice sources, just as he was, centuries later. Forts of past spice-seeking nations and monuments to their adventurers of bygone times constantly reminded Kaestner of the world's spice-laden past.

In this new system, McCormick set out to identify the best sources of spices from Africa to the East, setting up a dozen or more global sourcing operations with local shippers. These might take the form of joint ventures with local spice traders on the Malabar coast of western India or a legal relationship with a company already in operation. In Indonesia, for example, these arrangements involved collaborations with overland Chinese trading companies that had replaced the Dutch system or with Indonesian government officials in the Suharto government during the 1970s and 1980s. Cross-culturally, the overland Chinese, acting as merchants in another culture, had to leave a small footprint in conducting their trading. Since they were capitalist businessmen, they accrued a great deal of profit, and at times their lofty financial status resulted in a deep resentment among native Indonesians that could occasionally turn violent. In an effort to offset this threat, in many cases the Chinese changed their identities by assuming local Indonesian names, thus attempting to blend into a local community.

Working with regional merchants, McCormick began to dominate the retail spice market, providing products for both homes and restaurants. During the last half-century, in the United States and many other places across the globe, large food-producing chains have emerged to feed growing populations. Firms such as McDonald's, Kentucky Fried Chicken, Wendy's and Burger King, as well as massive food companies such as Kraft, General Foods and Pillsbury, now consume the great bulk of imported spices. Domestic use of spices still continues, but the greatest volume is consumed in the forms of the coatings for chicken, the mixes for hamburgers and the basic ingredients in the sauces and packaged products that fill the aisles of modern supermarkets. To confirm this, one needs only read the labels on cans, boxes and frozen products to see the wide distribution of spices in various products.

This evolution from home consumption to large-scale production caused McCormick to concentrate more on scientific approaches to spice development and marketing. There now had to be concern for the overall quality and purity of a spice that was put into products that were consumed by millions, if not billions, of people every hour of every day. As he moved through the sources of spices, Hank Kaestner saw how cinnamon was stripped from the barks of trees and cloves were sorted in the drying sun. He then had to determine what would have to be done to ensure the quality of these raw spices before they emerged in the marketplace. This might involve setting up small plants to assure cleanliness in all aspects of production, from washing hands to sorting out foreign matter found among the spices. Quality control was a major concern. This 'global sourcing' also involved finding local managers who could ensure quality and also identify and maintain the best sources for the spices. Competitively, this also meant an edge for McCormick in the global marketplace. Here the company could ensure both high quality and the best price by controlling the spice at its

Bee Brand vanilla advertisement. After their beginnings in the 1890s McCormick was shipping to South America, Europe, Africa and the East and West Indies through their New York export office.

source. Many major food companies that purchase spices for their product development buy them from McCormick, as they have done for decades.

While McCormick dominated the market, many smaller companies in Europe, Asia, Africa, Australia and the Americas continued to prosper, providing spices for various food and distribution markets in various regions of the world.

International Spice Trading Groups

In 1906, the publication of a book rocked the households of the United States. Upton Sinclair's *The Jungle* detailed the unsanitary conditions of meat-packing plants producing food for homes. The public outcry caused by the book led to national legislation to protect food safety. About a year later, a group of men met in New York City to form the American Spice Trade Association (ASTA). The opening statement of that meeting focused on connecting the spice trade to pure food legislation and upholding the Pure Food and Drug Act, recently passed by the US Congress. The nation was in shock from *The Jungle*, and these spice traders felt the waves of public outrage. So, for the 56 men attending that meeting, fear may have been a motivating factor: a fear of losing their businesses because of unhealthy conditions. However, in the early decades of its existence, the organization, consisting exclusively of traders in the United States, focused on the nitty-gritty world of contracts and arbitration as well as establishing a liaison with the Federal Government, which was enforcing pure food legislation.

The Great Depression of 1929 affected spices, as it did all markets, and ASTA struggled through many types of reorganization over the ensuing decades. During the 1970s there was more consciousness about the quality and purity of spices coupled with concern about government regulation as there had been seven decades earlier. Issues such as quality control, packaging, nutrition and sanitation were of paramount importance. In the 1980s the Chernobyl nuclear leaks and the waves of radioactive material that drifted across Europe instigated new fears of possible contamination of plants and products. Now questions were asked about sources of food and the conditions at the source. The 1990s brought new issues such as food safety and trans-fatty acid to the forefront. As the twenty-first century began, ASTA expanded its membership globally, including all international members who trade with the United States.

While ASTA is now an internationally inclusive organization in relation to American spice trading, many other global spice organizations exist that represent national, regional or individual spice products. The Canadians have their association; there are several in South Asia, Japan and Australia, and European countries such as Denmark, Italy, Germany and the United Kingdom have their own national groups.

Modern Issues in the Spice World

Looking at the website of one of the national spice associations can be an eye-opening experience as regards the myriad issues faced by spice traders and companies that market spices. Loaded terms such as 'methyl bromide', 'spice adulteration', 'workplace safety', 'ethylene oxide' and 'food additives' conjure up a plethora of negative images that at one point would never have crossed people's minds when they reached for a jar of spices in their supermarket.

The significance of the phrase 'workplace safety' is obvious, but spice adulteration has been an issue for centuries. The early European spice traders who moved in and out of the spice ports of Asia were ever on the lookout for suppliers who added other ingredients to the spice sack to increase its weight. Hard lessons were learned and sometimes resolved on the next trip. In the modern era, adulteration of spices takes a different tack. The essential questions become: does the label on the spice jar, or on the product that contains spices, state a spice as part of the product and, if so, is that spice actually contained in the product? If a hamburger mixture claims to have cloves and black pepper as part of the package, are they actually present or are they imitations of the real thing? Here, chemistry and science

Chillies hanging up to dry in China.

play a big role. Gone are the days when you emptied a sack of cloves from a ship and all the spikes and crowns of the cloves spilled out before you or you saw foreign elements that were mixed in to adulterate the spice.

The pesticide methyl bromide is applied as a liquid that vaporizes on crops. In the United Kingdom supermarkets such as the Co-op and Marks & Spencer have called for it to be phased out. Ethylene oxide is an industrial chemical used for fumigating spices in an effort to kill microorganisms that may harm the spice. When you consider that most spices are scraped off trees, piled on the ground and pulled off low bushes, there is reason for concern about small organisms affecting the spice. There have been suggestions of cancer risk as a result of ingesting such chemicals in food. In the United States, the Food and Drug Administration (FDA) analyses all these chemicals and additives and those that are not approved cannot be used. Since 1983 irradiation is increasingly used on spices, a process that kills contaminants without altering either the appearance or the taste of the spice. Human bodies take in hundreds of types of substances daily, and most are digested without any harm. At times the public becomes alarmed without knowing the facts about additives or processes. At other times problems can be found, and public relations nightmares can ensue. Nonetheless, one spice dealer recently asked the following (rhetorical) question about additives and spices: how much of an adverse effect can the chemicals on a few grains of pepper or a few cloves have, especially when compared to eating a steak or vegetables with comparable additives that may be consumed in much greater volume?

Organic Spices and Fair Trade

Various spice companies have moved to the development and marketing of organic spices. McCormick has introduced a full line of such spices for the marketplace. Big food chains in the US that sell in bulk to consumers such as Wal-Mart, BJ's, Sam's Club, Price Club and Costco are demanding more organic products for their customers. (And some food stores, such as Whole Foods and Trader Joe's, specialize in or have more organic than non-organic products on offer). In the United States such developments have been partially stimulated by the National Organic Program of the United States Department of Agriculture (USDA), which began in 2002. The USDA sends out agents to check on companies that are claiming to have developed organic goods. It is estimated that 5–10 per cent of agricultural products now marketed are organic.

In recent decades fair trade has emerged as a concept in the global marketplace. The basic idea applied to the spice trade might go like this: let's assume that US$1.50 is the cost

A spice market in Yemen at the base of the Arabian Peninsula.

of producing 1 pound of cloves. Cloves might sell at $1–2 a pound. If the market price goes to $2, the seller gets that amount, or a 50-cent profit. However, if the market price drops to $1 or lower, the seller always gets a minimum of $1.50, or the production cost.

Organic farming plays out in different ways. One spice wholesaler, Vermont-based ForesTrade, started in Sumatra, where the company founder, Thomas Fricke, was asked to identify incentives that would discourage commercial development of a local national park. Using cinnamon as a focus crop, Fricke demonstrated how local farmers could develop an organic spice without clearing large sections of land that would endanger this national park. The key was to market the cinnamon in Europe and North America to dealers who could pay a good price and thus reward the Sumatran farmers for their labour. This was not a simple process, since it involved a number of factors including a network between grower and wholesaler, which included community associations, individual entrepreneurs, businesses already in place and, importantly, local non-governmental organizations dedicated to protecting the environment. A complex network of people and organizations had to work together for a common goal. When it is successful, environmental sustainability and profit can go hand in hand. ForesTrade now collaborates with 6,000 indigenous producers in 200 communities in Indonesia and Guatemala. It is also creating alliances with others in Sri Lanka, India and Madagascar.

Another example of the evolution of fair trade practices involves the Salagama, a Hindu caste of people on primarily Buddhist Sri Lanka who traditionally peeled the cinnamon from the tree. Over the centuries that the Portuguese, Dutch and English sequentially controlled the cinnamon trade on this island, the Salagama were devastated by the mandatory payment of annual tributes, which grew sixfold when the Portuguese were there. Later, under British control, the death rates soared among these cinnamon workers. Frequently the Salagama would register their children under the names of another caste so that they could avoid the demanding labour imposed by these European colonists. In recent years, the situation has changed for some of these cinnamon workers, who now sell their products to a local fair trade association that can often get 40 per cent above the market rate for the sweetly perfumed harvest. These fair trade programmes seem to work if people are willing to pay just a little more for their spice products. Doing so improves the lives of those who labour to give us these spices and also helps erase centuries of human abuse.

Spices and Health

Spices have always been viewed as a source of healthy habits. But many of the old remedies to cure ills that originated in

Bhut Jolokia, the hottest chilli in the world, discovered in Northern India. It has over 1 million Scoville heat units.

the ancient and medieval worlds have gone by the wayside in the light of the scientific revolution and modern medicine. Still, even in today's world, there appear to be many positive health benefits of spices.

Cinnamon has been touted as a product that can lower cholesterol and regulate blood sugar, helping people with type 2 diabetes. Studies on yeast-infection prevention and even the reduction of the proliferation of leukaemia and lymphoma cancer have involved cinnamon. In Denmark research on arthritis prevention showed that cinnamon offered relief. The spice may also inhibit bacterial growth and food spoilage as well as fighting *E. coli* bacteria in unpasteurized juices. Studies also show that, beside being a good source of calcium, iron, fibre and manganese, cinnamon may also boost cognitive function and memory.

The cayenne pepper of the Americas has been touted as a nutritional and medicinal spice that has positive effects on both the digestive and circulatory systems of the body. For the digestive system, it helps the body create hydrochloric acid, which is necessary for good digestion. It has even been known to stop heart attacks. There have also been suggestions that it can be beneficial for acne, coughs, colds, low blood pressure and tumours. One doctor has even employed it to cure a toothache, while another finds that it increases energy.

One factor that should be kept in mind about spices is that many of them do lose their effectiveness after a period of time. Spice merchants like Ian Hemphill of Herbie's Spices in Sydney, Australia, place a 'best before' date on their spice packages. McCormick promotes ads that say, 'If you see Baltimore, MD, on the label, the spice is at least 15 years old.' They even have an informative page on their website about the ageing of different spices.

Spices, Culture and History

In many areas of the world where the climate is hot, the spices used are also hot. In southern India, Mexico and parts of Africa, many dishes are served with spices that will burn your tongue and bring sweat to your brow. The flavours of the Arab world are blends of spices that will awaken your appetite in the heat, but not deny you the moisture needed in these arid and desert lands. I grew up with a diet of bland German cooking. Some food preparations I liked, others I dreaded eating. It never dawned on me why my mother's dishes were the way they were. My experiences at boarding schools in upper elementary school, high school and college were not much different. Spaghetti with red tomato sauce may have been the height of my spicy experience during these growing years. Only in adulthood did I begin to visit cities and experience foods and spices of different global cultures. I liked it. From that point forward I was hooked on spices.

About a decade ago a study was published in the United States that explained a lot about cultures and their use of spices. The study showed that after analysing the cuisines of 36 nations, based on 4,578 'traditional' recipes from 93 cook-books, it was found that the hotter and wetter a nation, the spicier its food would be. The authors of the study, Jennifer Billing and Paul Sherman, concluded that as the risk of food spoilage grows, so does a dependence on spices which are a natural antimicrobial source. So, more spices, less a chance of having those small bugs upset your stomach and health.

The survey further showed that about 93 per cent of all surveyed recipes used at least one spice. Each recipe from Ethiopia, Kenya, Greece, India, Indonesia, Iran, Malaysia, Morocco, Nigeria and Thailand was spiced. When the food of nations in northern Europe such as Finland and Norway was studied, spices were found in no more than one recipe in three. One powerful result of this study focused on the spice-eating habits of the Japanese and Koreans who live in fairly close proximity at similar latitudes. Koreans, were 50 per cent more likely than the Japanese to use spices in their food, with the result that the Japanese experienced more food-poisoning incidents than Koreans. For the Koreans it was three people in 100,000, for the Japanese, 30.

Spices Go Global

It seems that spices have reached their ultimate level of maturity, wherein their use is diversified across all the continents and in many commercial fields far beyond food. British skincare and cosmetics emporium, Molton Brown, offers black pepper eau de toilette, body wash and shower gel, which mixes the spice with ginger, cumin and coriander for a result that is 'masculine, but not overpowering'. The first scent developed by Jo Malone of London, an exclusive connoisseur and retailer of fragrances, candles and related products, was nutmeg and ginger, still one of her most popular creations.

Today, urban centres and small towns alike across the globe offer a wide array of ethnic restaurants whose dishes reflect the history of spices over the last millennium. No longer are major cities such as New York, London, Amsterdam and Singapore the primary venues for food from Burma, Mexico, India, Tibet and Thailand. In a world where immigrants hail from far and wide, with more and more Asians settling in the West, most likely more and more of their foodstuffs will be available in shops and eateries.

Down through the centuries, the ultimate mixture of spices has been found in curries, which are a mixture of meat, fish, vegetables, or fruit with a spice mixture. The spice mixture that comes to us from India is called masala, which is a pre-prepared blending of various spices. A garam masala may contain a mixture of black pepper, cinnamon and cloves. Also of Indian origin is the type of dish known as vindaloo, which has Portuguese roots as well, following those European colonists' times on the Malabar coast, where cooking with meat or fish was done in wine vinegar and garlic. Indians may prepare similar dishes using mustard oil, ghee (melted butter) and/or lard to cook the meat, adding garlic and then

A German spice plant advertising card (*c.* 1912) showing cinnamon stalks being gathered. Sticky cinnamon buns (*Schnecken*, 'snails') are a favourite treat in Germany.

the major ingredient, chilli, which gives the vindaloo a spicy heat. Curries and their various related dishes are ongoing global and local variations of cross-cultural encounters.

Other spice blendings have taken place in various cultures. The British have, over time, developed pickling spice, a combination of allspice, cloves, mace, chillies, coriander, mustard seeds and ginger. A pudding spice called Mixed Spice for use in biscuits, desserts and cakes has also evolved in Britain; it contains cinnamon, cloves, mace, nutmeg, coriander and allspice. One famous American mixture is cajun seasoning, which makes extensive use of cayenne and black pepper.

Ian Hemphill, the Australian spice author and dealer writes of many native plants that enrich the foods of his continent. Among them is wattleseed which comes from acacia trees bearing leguminous seed pods. One type of acacia is the Mulga tree which grows in the outback to heights of 6 metres. The Aborigines ate these seeds for protein, but for use as a spice they should be roasted and ground. When ground the spice resembles ground coffee and has a light, coffee-like aroma and a slightly bitter, nutty, coffee taste. This spice is used to flavour sweet dishes such as ice cream, yogurt, cheesecakes and whipped cream. It is also used in pancakes, goes well with breads and complements chicken, lamb and fish when used in small amounts. Hemphill and his spice partner and wife Elizabeth, who run a spice store in Sydney, employ native ingredients with traditional spices. He outlines his efforts in one of his books, *Spice Notes*. Cultural blendings affected the European powers in the geographic areas they encountered although, historically, the Portuguese at home have made little use of the spices they once desired so strongly. This is less true of the Dutch, who have incorporated spices in a number of their main dishes and desserts. The *rijsttafel* is a combination of plates of meat dishes that are either in a stew or presented on a skewer as satay and represent the cultural areas of Sumatra, Bali and Java, all major venues of the Dutch spice empire (and colonization). The abundance of Indonesian restaurants in Amsterdam and other Dutch cities and towns also reflects their history of spices. The British have adopted curries as a result of their experience in colonial India. Some dishes, according to Lizzie Collingham in her history, *Curry*, such as chicken tikka masala, have become a new national dish for Great Britain. Some critics say, however, that many of the 'Indian' dishes that are consumed outside the subcontinent in Indian restaurants are very distant relatives of the dishes the Indians themselves prepare and eat. The same is often said of the fare offered in many Chinese eateries throughout the West, especially the ubiquitous takeaway restaurants.

So check your jars and boxes of spices and other foods at home and at the supermarket, ask questions at restaurants about spice ingredients, search the Internet for sources of spices and for recipes using different types of these flavourings, each with its own world history. Spices are with you and around you and in you. Experiment with them, enjoy them, and think of the journey they made over the miles and the centuries to get to your table and your palate!

Glossary

Sugar and spice and everything nice,
that's what little girls are made of.
Nursery rhyme

There are many plants that can be classified as spices. This glossary focuses on the spices that have a global reach. For further research you might want to consider such spices as caraway, zedoary, asafetida, juniper, galangal, nigella, poppy, cubeb, sumac, ajowan, fenugreek, wasabi, pomegranate, mahlab, screwpine, curry leaf, mango powder and kaffir lime.

Alleppey Pepper: A type of Malabar pepper from the state of Kerala on the Malabar Coast of south-west India with a good harbour on the Arabian Sea. Alleppey was historically the name given to Malabar pepper grown in the southern part of the state of Kerala.

Allspice: This spice, which is from the West Indies and Central and South America, is a small bushy tree of the myrtle family. Columbus brought it back to Europe thinking it was pepper. Its Spanish name is *pimienta* or pepper. Like chilli pepper it is a unique New World spice. Allspice is primarily used in the food industry in pickles, sausages, ketchup and canning meat. It can be also used as a spiced tea mix, in soups and curries and as a pickling spice.

Anise: This spice is related to caraway, cumin, dill and fennel. It is a native of some islands of the Eastern Mediterranean and the Middle East. During the Middle Ages it was cultivated all over Europe. It has been historically used as a digestive, especially after consuming a large meal. Anise is also good for freshening the breath, with its liquorice-like taste, and is used in a number of alcoholic drinks such as the French *anisette*, the Turkish *raki*, the South American *aguardiente*, and Pernod. It is also used in the Middle East and India in soups and stews.

Banda and Amboina: The two Spice Islands in the Moluccas where nutmeg was principally grown during the competition between the Dutch and Portuguese for control of the spice trade.

Black Pepper: This is prepared by drying the immature berry. It had its origins on the Malabar Coast of south-western India.

Brazilian Black Pepper: This pepper is grown in the Belem area in the state of Para. It has a lower oil content than Indian and Indonesian pepper.

Brazilian White Pepper: This pepper is lighter in colour than Muntok and some consider it to have a bland flavour.

Cardamom: This spice historically grew wild in the rainforest areas of southern India and Sri Lanka. Today it is also grown in East Africa, Central America and Vietnam. It is an ancient spice highly valued in Indian culture and was used by the Romans and Greeks for digestion, perfume and as a breath freshener. Ancient Egyptians used it as a whitener for teeth. It has a smell like camphor and lemon and is a main ingredient in garam masala. In Arab cultures it is used in coffee and in Scandinavia found in spiced breads and pastries.

Cassia: This is similar to cinnamon but different in quality. Cassia bark is darker and thicker with a coarse, cork-like outer bark. It is less expensive than cinnamon and is often sold as cinnamon.

When buying sticks of cinnamon and cassia note that cinnamon rolls into a single quill while cassia is rolled from both sides toward the centre. Cassia is native to Burma and is also grown throughout South and South East Asia, the East and West Indies and Central America.

Chilli Pepper: There are many varieties of chilli peppers. The most common, *Capsicum annuum*, includes bell peppers, paprika and jalapeños. *Capsicum frutescens* include cayenne and tabasco while *chinense* identifies the hottest peppers such as habaneros and Scotch Bonnets. Others such as *pubescens* cover South American rocoto peppers and *baccatum* includes the South American aji pepper.

Cinnamon: This spice is indigenous to the island of Sri Lanka (Ceylon). It comes from the bark of an evergreen tree of the laurel family.

Clove: The clove is native to the North Moluccas, often called the Spice Islands, which are part of present-day Indonesia. Today it is cultivated in Brazil, the West Indies, Mauritius, Madagascar, India, Sri Lanka, Zanzibar and Pemba.

Coriander: Originally from the Eastern Mediterranean and mentioned in ancient Egypt and the Bible, it is now cultivated worldwide in Eastern Europe, the Middle East, India, Iran, the United States and Central America. The green leaves of the plant are herbs and the white or pink flowers develop into the spice seed which is ground up for use in curries, meats, pickling spice and for baking. In France it is used in vegetable dishes such as *à la grecque*. The oil derived from the seed is used to flavour chocolate and other drinks.

Cumin: Cumin, a plant similar in size to coriander, originated in the Nile valley and quickly spread to other areas of North Africa and on to Asia Minor and then east to Iran, India, Indonesia and China. In its northern migration from Africa it was grown in Spain and then taken to the Americas. It is mostly grown in warm latitudes but can also be grown as far north as Norway. Like coriander, cumin is essential to Indian cooking and, like cardamom, it is used in garam masala. In Germany and France cumin is used in cakes and breads and the Dutch and Swiss use it in cheese. It can be used in perfumes and the liqueur, kummel, uses it as a flavouring.

Ginger: One of the oldest spices known, ginger was cultivated in tropical Asia. Confucius mentions it in his writings in the fifth century BCE. It was well known in ancient Egypt, Greece and Rome. It is rich in vitamin C and was used by Chinese sailors to ward off scurvy. By the end of the first century CE it was widely used in Europe. During the Age of Exploration it was taken to West Africa by the Portuguese, to East Africa by the Arabs and to the New World by the Spanish. The ginger root, or rhizome, travels well and today it is grown in most tropical regions. For fresh ginger, the rhizome root is scraped or ground after washing and drying. For preserved ginger the rhizome is soaked in brine and put in a syrup. Dried ginger is boiled and peeled before drying. In Asian dishes ginger is often mixed with garlic. It is used in curry powder and in cakes, puddings and cookies and in Asian vegetable dishes. Ginger beer and wine are popular in some cultures. To 'ginger up' in English means to liven up your life.

Over 100 years ago W. M. Gibbs, a spice-loving author, penned these lines to express his fondness for ginger:

> Ginger black or ginger white
> Will furnish warmth in coldest night
> Without ginger how many would miss
> A ginger cookie for little Sis.

Green Pepper: This is from the immature black pepper plant: the peppercorns are harvested before they mature and are either allowed to dry or bottled in vinegar, brine or water. They offer a fresher flavour and are less pungent than either white or black pepper.

Guinea Pepper: Another name for 'grains of paradise', used because of its origin in West Africa. It has been also called 'malagueta pepper'. It is very pungent and has a biting taste. Before the Portuguese came to India and Malabar pepper became more easily available in Europe, the West African coast was known as the 'pepper coast'.

Herbs: These are plants that do not have a woody stem and die at the end of each growing season.

Lampong Black Pepper: From the south-eastern section of the island of Sumatra which serves as a principal centre for pepper production in Indonesia. It is also known as *acheen* or Sumatra pepper.

Lemon Grass: Found throughout South and South East Asia, it was used in ancient South Asian Ayurvedic medicine and has long been a staple spice in South East Asian cooking, especially in Malay, Indonesian and Thai dishes. Emitting a fresh lemon taste, it is used in soups and stews. It goes well with fish and poultry and is also found in soaps, detergents, perfumes and toiletries for its lemon aroma.

Long Black Pepper: From Southern India on the Deccan plain north-east of the Malabar Coast. In ancient Rome it was the most favoured pepper compared with the Malabar.

Mace: The lacy red covering over the brown nutmeg which is called *aril*. When it is pulled off the nut and broken into parts the mace is called 'blades'. For every 100 pounds of nutmeg produced only a single pound of mace will be gathered. Mace is therefore more valuable. Its flavour is sweeter and much stronger than that of the nutmeg. Mace dries lighter in colour and as such is used in dishes where the dark pieces of the nutmeg are not desired.

Malabar Black Pepper: Pepper from the Malabar area of south-west India in the state of Kerala. A general term used for both alleppey and tellicherry pepper.

Muntok Black Pepper: Named after a seaport on the south-east side of Sumatra.

Muntok White Pepper: This is produced on the island of Bangka in Indonesia and is exported from Muntok. It has a mild flavour.

Nutmeg: This spice is native to the Banda Islands of Indonesia and grows as an evergreen tree which can be as high as 20 metres (65 feet). It is also grown in the Caribbean, especially on the island of Grenada.

Penang Black Pepper: From an island 2½ miles off the west coast of the Malay Peninsula formally known as Prince of Wales Island, which is part of the Malaysian state of Penang. It was the first British settlement in Malaya. Penang is used in many Malay dishes such as Black Pepper Chicken. Pepper mixes usually contain Malabar for weight, Penang for strength and Sumatra for colour.

Pink Peppercorns: They are not true peppercorns but come from the dried fruit of the baies or poivre rose. They have a sweet pepper flavour and are used a great deal in French cooking.

Piper Retrofractum: Similar to long pepper from southern India but grown in South East Asia and mostly cultivated in Indonesia and Thailand. Often this black pepper is not distinguished from its Indian relative.

Saffron: Without question this is the most expensive spice in the world. Out of 100,000 to 250,000 handpicked plants, 1 pound of saffron is yielded. First found in the Near East in Asia Minor it was used by the Persians as both a flavouring and dye. The blue-violet and lily shaped flowers of the plant appear in autumn. At the centre of these flowers are three blood-red stigmas, which are the saffron threads that form the spice. It is better to buy the stigma rather than powdered saffron because the powder may be already mixed with other ingredients. Saffron is a strong feature in French bouillabaisse, Italian risotto and Spanish paella and features its aroma, bitter flavour and colour. Very little should be used, not only because of the expense, but because too much will emit a medicinal taste. In Indian cooking it is used in pilafs and biryani dishes. Saffron can also be found on the foreheads of Indian women denoting their caste.

Sarawak Pepper: This pepper has a unique taste, favoured by many chefs around the world. Some describe it as a 'toasty' flavour with winey, pungent tones. The white pepper has a uniform colour and a bolder taste than its black counterpart. These peppers are grown on the north-west side of the island of Borneo and constitute over 90 per cent of Malaysian pepper, which is mostly shipped to British Commonwealth countries.

Spice: The aromatic part of a tropical plant, be it root, bark, flower or seed. Most spices are of Asian origin with chilli pepper, vanilla and allspice being exceptions.

Spice Islands: Also called the Moluccas, they are a group of islands in East Indonesia between the island of Celebes and New Guinea. They are composed of three large islands, several smaller island groups and even smaller islands, among them Ambon, Ternate and Tidore, which were major sites of the spice wars.

Sri Lankan Black Pepper: This is a grey-black pepper and is much bolder than Lampong black pepper.

Tamarind: This tree is native to tropical Africa and grows wild throughout the Sudan. It was introduced to India so long ago that many think it is native to that area of South Asia. It was popular with the Arabs in the Middle Ages and the Crusaders probably introduced it into Europe because it was a good thirst quencher. The fruit is in the form of curved pods that turn brown when ripe. It is used as a souring agent, as lemon or lime might be, in India and South East Asia, and in many cultures it is used as a mild laxative. Tamarind is commonly mixed with sugar and water in the American tropics as a cooling drink. Its pulp is used to flavour preserves and chutney, to make meat sauces and to pickle fish. Sweets can also be made from the pulp by mixing it with dry sugar and forming the mixture into different shapes. A slab of tamarind can be employed as a brass and copper polish by adding some salt and then wetting the mixture to shine the metals. During the British occupation of India, the British soldiers would put a fresh tamarind in their ear when entering native areas to protect themselves. People in south-west India believed that the fresh pods were inhabited by demons and thus avoided the soldiers who were wearing them.

Tellicherry Black Pepper: A black pepper grown in north-west Kerala on the south-western Malabar coast of India, as opposed to alleppey, from the southern part of Malabar. The British East India Company established a factory here in 1683. Tellicherry berries are very large and regular in size and usually commands a higher price than other Malabar pepper. Italian sausage makers prefer it for making salami since the pepper is strongly flavoured and has a distinctive appearance.

Turmeric: Part of the ginger family. It grows in warm wet climates and was once a highly valued alternative to saffron as a colouring. Today its musky flavour is primarily used in curry powders and its golden colour to dye the robes of Buddhist monks. Historically it has also had a mystical side in some Pacific islands where it was worn as a protective charm to keep away evil spirits. In India turmeric is used with fish, eggs, poultry and meat, as well as in curries. The western world uses its musky and bitter flavour in preserves and some mustards, relishes and salad dressings.

Vanilla: Vanilla is native to Central America, southern Mexico and the West Indies. The Spanish conquistadores Cortés and Diaz first noted its use among the Aztecs. Cortés took both vanilla and cocoa back to Spain. Soon Europeans began using vanilla in their chocolate beverages. Some Europeans attempted to grow vanilla in greenhouses but such attempts failed. In the nineteenth century it was discovered that vanilla beans, growing on their climbing tropical vines, were pollinated by bees and other insects native to Mexico. Charles Morren, a Belgian, discovered how to artificially fertilize vanilla in 1836. From that point the French started raising vanilla on their islands of Madagascar and Reunion off the East African coast. An American invented vanilla extract which was utilized in baking, custards and puddings as well as in ice cream. Most of the vanilla sold today is in the form of extract or is synthetic. However, vanilla beans, those long wrinkly, dark brown strips, are quite versatile and can be rinsed and reused countless times, even after soaking in milk or a sauce. Vanilla beans can be kept in a jar of sugar; this will flavour the sugar as well as keeping the bean available for future use.

White Pepper: White pepper is prepared by removing the mesocarp that is the middle or fleshy layer of the fruit wall. It is mostly used in sauces, mayonnaise and cream soups where a dark colour is not desired.

Select Bibliography

Books About Spices

American Spice Trade Association, *A Glossary of Spices* (New York, 1966)

Claiborne, Craig, *Cooking with Herbs and Spices* (New York, 1963)

Daisley, Gilda, *The Illustrated Book of Herbs* (London, 1985)

Day, Avanelle and Lillie Stuckey, *The Spice Book* (New York, 1964)

Divakaruni, Chitra Banerjee, *The Mistress of Spices* (New York, 1997)

Doole, Louise Evans, *Herb Magic and Garden Craft* (New York, 1972)

Gibbs, W. M., *Spices and How to Know Them* (Buffalo, NY, 1909)

Greenberg, Sheldon and Elisabeth Lambert Ortiz, *The Spice of Life* (New York, 1984)

Grieve, Mrs M., *A Modern Herbal*, vol. II, (New York, 1971)

Hemphill, Ian, *Spice Notes* (Sydney, 2000)

Hemphill, Ian and Kate, *The Spice and Herb Bible* (Toronto, 2002)

Hemphill, Rosemary, *The Penguin Book of Herbs and Spices* (London, 1966)

Humphrey, Sylvia Windle, *A Matter of Taste: The Definitive Seasoning Cookbook* (New York, 1965)

James, Wendy and Clare Pumfrey, *Cooking with Herbs and Spices* (London, 1976)

Lang, Jenifer Harvey, ed., *Larousse Gastronomique* (New York, 1984)

McCormick & Company, *Spices of the World Cookbook* (New York, 1964)

McGee, Harold, *On Food and Cooking* (Boston, MA, 1984)

Miloradovich, Milo, *The Art of Cooking with Herbs and Spices* (Garden City, NY, 1950)

Norman, Jill, *Spices, Roots and Fruits* (London, 1989)

—, *Spices, Seeds and Barks* (London, 1989)

—, *Herbs and Spices* (New York, 2002)

—, *The Complete Book of Spices* (New York, 1991)

Ripperger, Helmut, *Spice Cookery* (New York, 1942)

Root, Waverley, ed., *Food: An Authoritative and Visual History and Dictionary of the Foods of the World* (New York, 1980)

—, *Herbs and Spices: A Guide to Culinary Seasoning* (New York, 1985)

Rosengarten, Frederic Jr, *The Book of Spices* (Wynnewood, PA, 1969)

Schuler, Stanley, ed., *Simon & Schuster's Guide to Herbs and Spices* (New York, 1990)

Stobart, Tom, *Herbs, Spices and Flavorings* (Woodstock, NY, 1970)

Swahn, J. O., *The Lore of Spices* (New York, 1991)

Thomas, Gertrude Z., *Richer than Spices: How a Royal Bride's Dowry Introduced Cane, Lacquer, Cottons, Tea, and Porcelain to England, and So Revolutionized Taste, Manners, Craftsmanship, and History in Both England and America* (New York, 1965)

Tidbury, G. E., *The Clove Tree* (London, 1949)

Woodward, Marcus, *Gerard's Herball* (London, 1927)

SPICES IN WORLD HISTORY

Andrews, Kenneth R., *Trade, Plunder, and Settlement: Maritime Enterprise and the Genesis of the British Empire 1480–1630* (New York, 1984)

Arasaratnam, Sinnappah, *Merchants, Companies and Commerce on the Coromandel Coast 1650–1740* (New Delhi, 1986)

Boxer, C. R., *The Dutch Seaborne Empire, 1600–1800* (London, 1965)

—, *The Portuguese Seaborne Empire, 1415–1825* (New York and London, 1969)

Braudel, Fernand, *The Mediterranean and the Mediterranean World in the Age of Philip II*, vols I and II (New York, 1966)

—, *The Structures of Everyday Life*, vol. I of *Civilization and Capitalism, 15th–18th Century* (New York, 1979)

—, *The Wheels of Commerce*, vol. II of *Civilization and Capitalism, 15th–18th Century* (New York, 1979)

—, *The Perspective of the World*, vol. III of *Civilization and Capitalism, 15th–18th Century* (New York, 1979)

Brierley, Joanna Hall, *Spices: The Story of Indonesia's Spice Trade* (New York, 1994)

Brothwell, Don and Patricia, *Food in Antiquity: A Survey of the Diet of Early Peoples* (New York, 1969)

Brotton, Jerry, *Trading Territories: Mapping the Early Modern World* (Ithaca, NY, 1998)

—, *The Renaissance Bazaar: From the Silk Road to Michelangelo* (New York, 2002)

Carr, Lois, Russell Menard and Lorena Wilson, *Robert Cole's World: Agriculture and Society in Early Maryland* (Chapel Hill, NC, 1991)

Corn, Charles, *The Scents of Eden: A Narrative of the Spice Trade* (New York, 1998)

Crosby, Alfred W., *The Columbian Exchange: Biological and Cultural Consequences of 1492* (Westport, CT, 1972)

Curtin, Philip D., *Cross-Cultural Trade in World History* (New York, 1984)

Dalby, Andrew, *Dangerous Tastes: The Story of Spices* (London and Berkeley, CA, 2000)

Dodge, Bertha S., *Plants That Changed the World* (Boston, MA, 1959)

—, *Quest for Spices and New Worlds* (Hamden, CT, 1988)

Dunn, Ross E., *The Adventures of Ibn Battuta, a Muslim Traveller of the 14th Century* (Berkeley, CA, 1986)

Dupree, Nathalie, *Nathalie Dupree's Matters of Taste* (New York, 1990)

Faas, Patrick, *Around the Roman Table: Food and Feasting in Ancient Rome* (New York, 2003)

Fernández-Armesto, Felipe, *Pathfinders: A Global History of Exploration* (New York, 2006)

Foster, Sir William, *England's Quest of Eastern Trade* (London, 1966)

Frank, Andre Gunder, *Reorient: Global Economy in the Asian Age* (Berkeley, CA, 1998)

Freedman, Paul, *Spices and the Medieval Imagination* (New Haven, CT, 2008)

Hall, Clayton, *Narratives of Early Maryland* (Annapolis, MD, 1967)

Heiser, Charles B. Jr, *Seed to Civilization, The Story of Food* (Cambridge, MA, 1990)

—, *Of Plants and People* (Norman, OK, 1985)

Hobhouse, Henry, *Forces of Change: Why We Are the Way We Are Now* (London, 1989)

Hourani, Albert, *A History of the Arab Peoples* (Cambridge, MA, 1991)

Jardine, Lisa, *Worldly Goods: A New History of the Renaissance* (New York, 1996)

Keay, John, *The Spice Route: A History* (London, 2005)

Lane, Frederic C., *Venice: A Maritime Republic* (Baltimore, MD, 1973)

Lattimore, Owen and Eleanor, *Silks, Spices and Empire: Asia through the Eyes of Its Discoverers* (New York, 1968)

Masselman, George, *The Cradle of Colonialism* (New Haven, CT, 1963)

Miller, J. Innes, *The Spice Trade of the Roman Empire, 29 BC to AD 641* (New York, 1969)

Milton, Giles, *Nathaniel's Nutmeg: Or, The True and Incredible Adventures of the Spice Trader Changed the Course of History* (New York, 1999)

Parry, J. H., *The Age of Reconnaissance: Discovery, Exploration, and Settlement, 1450–1650* (New York, 1963)

—, *The Spanish Seaborne Empire* (New York, 1966)

—, *The Discovery of the Sea: An Illustrated History of Men, Ships and the Sea in the Fifteenth and Sixteenth Centuries* (Berkeley CA, 1974)

Pearson, M. N., ed., *Spices in the Indian Ocean World* (Brookfield, VT, 1996)

Penrose, Boies, *Travel and Discovery in the Renaissance, 1420–1620* (New York, 1975)

Prakash, Om, ed., *European Commercial Expansion in Early Modern Asia* (Brookfield, VT, 1996)

Prestage, Edgar, *The Portuguese Pioneers* (London, 1966)

Putnam, George Granville, *Salem Vessels and Their Voyages* (Salem, MA, 1922)

Ritchie, Carson I. A., *Food in Civilization, How History Has Been Affected by Human Tastes* (New York, 1981)

Russell-Wood, A.J.R., *The Portuguese Empire, 1415–1808* (Baltimore, MD, 1998)

Schivelbusch, Wolfgang, *Tastes of Paradise: A Social History of Spices, Stimulants and Intoxicants* (New York, 1992)

Schurz, William Lytle, *The Manila Galleon* (New York, 1949)

Sheriff, Abdul, *Slaves, Spices and Ivory in Zanzibar: Integration of an East African Commercial Empire into the World Economy, 1770–1873* (Athens, OH, 1987)

Simoons, Frederick J., *Food in China: A Cultural and Historical Inquiry* (Boca Raton, FL, 1991)

Spicing up the Palate: Studies of Flavourings – Ancient and Modern, Proceedings of the Oxford Symposium on Food and Cookery (1992)

Tannahill, Reay, *Food in History* (New York, 1973)

Thomas, Gertrude Z., *Richer than Spices* (New York, 1965)

Toussaint, Auguste, *History of the Indian Ocean* (Chicago, IL, 1966)

Turner, Jack, *Spice: The History of a Temptation* (New York, 2004)

Van den Boogaart, Ernst, *Civil and Corrupt Asia* (Chicago, IL, 2003)

Wallace, Alfred Russel, *The Malay Archipelago: The Land of the Orang-Utan and the Bird of Paradise* (London, 1902)

Welch, Jeanie M., compiler, *The Spice Trade: A Bibliographic Guide to Sources of Historical and Economic Information* (London, 1994)

Wolf, Eric R., *Europe and the People without History* (Berkeley, CA, 1982)

Zandvliet, Kees, ed., *The Dutch Encounter with Asia, 1600–1950*, exh. cat., Rijksmuseum, Amsterdam (Zwolle, 2002)

ARTICLES

Billing, J. and P. W. Sherman, 'Antimicrobial Functions of Spices: Why Some Like it Hot', *The Quarterly Review of Biology*, 73 (March 1998)

Clarence-Smith, William Gervase, 'Editorial – Islamic History as Global History', *Journal of Global History*, 2/part 2 (July 2007), p. 131ff.

De Vos, Paula, 'The Science of Spices: Empiricism and Economic Botany in the Early Spanish Empire', *Journal of World History*, 17/4 (December 2006)

McCants, Anne E. C., 'Exotic Goods, Popular Consumption, and the Standard of Living: Thinking About Globalizatin in the Early Modern World', *Journal of World History*, XVIII/4 (December 2007)

Seabrook, John, 'Soldiers and Spice', Letters From Indonesia, *The New Yorker* (13 August 2001), p. 60ff.

Smith, Stefan Halikowski, 'Perceptions of Nature in Early Modern Portuguese India', *Itinerario*, 2 (2007), pp. 17ff

Subrahmanyam, Sanjay, 'The Birth-pangs of Portuguese Asia: Revisiting the Fateful "Long Decade", 1498–1509', *Journal of Global History*, II/3 (November 2007), pp. 261ff

INTERVIEW WITH THE AUTHOR

Hank Kaesner, retired global trader for McCormick & Company, 3 May 2007

WIDENING YOUR SPICE WORLD

In writing *Spices: A Global History*, I have collected information from a wide array of printed sources, from ancient accounts to contemporary histories, which are acknowledged in the bibliography. Though I explored the Internet and was able to select and verify some fascinating facts gleaned from it, I would warn readers to take care not to get so tangled up in the World Wide Web as to overlook conventional printed matter, cinema and other audio and visual arts, such as the folk music of the Culture Music Club album *Spices of Zanzibar* or the films *Mirch Masala* (1985), which centers on pepper factory workers in India; *A Touch of Spice* (2003), about a young Greek boy whose grandfather has a spice shop in Istanbul; and the 2005 adaptation of the novel *The Mistress of Spices*.

Salman Rushdie's *The Moor's Last Sigh* tells a story of spice families on the Malabar Coast of India over 100 years ago. Frank Herbert's *Dune* explores the role of spices in a science-fiction world. Poetry is another avenue of exploration: John Dryden's 'Amboyna', 'Astraea Redux' and the multi-versed 'Annus Mirabilis' call to trade and spices. In the Romantic period you can read 'Little Derwent's Breakfast' by Emily Trevenen. In recent years, there is the poetry of Michael Ondaatje, including the sensual poem 'The Cinnamon Peeler.' Timothy Morton devotes a whole book to *The Poetics of Spice*. Lastly, there is travel, through which one can directly experience spices in a variety of contexts, sometimes even their original ones, as well as re-create the voyages taken by the early spice traders.

Spice Companies

The Americas

McCormick and Company
Sparks, Maryland
mccormick.com

McCormick in Canada is called Club House and in the UK, Schwartz. It is McCormick Foods in Australia, and Ducros in France, which is the largest spice company in Europe. It is also in Central America as McCormick de Centro America and in India as AVT McCormick. It is also in Mexico, Venezuela, Shanghai, Japan and Finland.

Penzey's Spices
Brookfield, Wisconsin
penzeys.com

Watkins Spices
Winona, Minnesota and Winnipeg, Canada
watkinsonline.com

The Great American Spice Company
Ft. Wayne, Indiana
americanSpice.com

American Spice Company
americanspice.us
Miami, Florida

Fuchs North America (formerly Baltimore Spice)
Owings Mills, Maryland
fuchsnorthamerica.com

The Great Spice Company (organic)
San Marcos, California
greatspice.com

Pacific Natural Spices
Commerce, California
pacspice.com

The Spice Hunter
San Luis Obispo, California
spicehunter.com

The Spice House
(Hermann Laue Spice Co. Inc.)
Ontario, Canada
thespicehouse.com

Spice Barn
Lewis Center, Ohio
spicebarn.com

Spice Islands
spiceislands.com

South Asia

Go to indiamart.com for a more detailed listing of South Asian spice companies. Selected companies are listed below.

Surendraray and Company
Mumbai, India
kamdarspices.com

Hindustan Global
Navi Mumbai, India
indiamart.com/hindustanglobal

National Masala Mills
New Delhi, India
kanwalspices.com

Spice Trade
Noida, India
spice-trade.com/products

About South Asian Spices

Peacock Spice Company
Royal Oak, Michigan
peacockspices.com

East Asia

Go to made-in-china.com for a detailed listing of spice companies.

S&B Foods
Tokyo, Japan
sbfoods.co.jp/eng/

Indonesia

PT Ruby Privatindo
Jakarta, Indonesia
Rubyndo.com

Q-Spicing
Jawa Barat, Indonesia
q-spicing.com

Singapore

Wee Kiat Development Pte
Singapore
spicescommodities.com

Vietnam

Vietnam Agro-Products Company
Ho Chi Min City and Hanoi, Vietnam
www.alibaba.com

UK and Europe

Alakh Indian Spices
Leicester, UK
pureindianspice.co.uk

Bart Spices
Bristol, UK
bartspices.com

Ducros
France
ducros.fr

Shropshire Spices

Shropshire, UK

shropshire-spice.co.uk

European Spice Services

Temse, Belgium

spices.be

Africa

Cape Herb and Spice Company

Capetown, South Africa

capeherb.com

About African Spices:

Mozambique Spice Company

Laguna Beach, California

mozambiquespicecompany.com

African Hut

Laguna Niguel, California

africanhut.com

My Spicer.com

Denver, CO

myspicer.com

Monterey Bay Spice Company

(African Bird Pepper)

www.herbco.com

Australia and New Zealand

Gregg's
Auckland, New Zealand
greggs.co.nz

Herbie's Spices
Sydney, Australia
herbies.com.au

Spice Organizations

The American Spice Traders Association
astaspice.org

Indian Spice Board
indianspices.com

International Pepper Community
ipcnet.org

European Spice Association
esa-spices.org

The Seasoning and Spice Association
seasoningandspice.org.uk

Canadian Spice Association
canadianspiceassociation.com

The Spice Council of Sri Lanka
srilankaspices.org

Spices Board of India
indianspices.com

Acknowledgements

Looking back over the decades, I want to thank my buddy Andy for all the times we sought out bookstores in cities and towns before and after our international education meetings and had those great discussions about history and food and how to research, write, and teach about food history and the roles that spices played. Many thanks also to Patricia Bayer for her helpful editorial comments and to Nancy Selden for fine work on developing the maps. Finally, to my wife, Betty, for her patience during the time it took to put all of this together in a coherent form.

Photo Acknowledgements

The author and publishers wish to express their thanks to the below sources of illustrative material and/or permission to reproduce it. Locations of some artworks are also given below.

Photo Alinari/Rex Features: p. 49; photo © Xavi Arnau/2008 iStock International, Inc.: p. 6; photo by the author: p. 116; Biblioteca Casanatense, Rome: p. 68; Bibliotheca Estense Universitaria, Modena: p. 46; Bibliothèque Nationale de France, Paris: p. 18; Bibliothèque Royale de Belgique, Bruxelles/Koninklijke Bibliotheek van België, Brussel: p. 63; Bridgeman Art Archive: pp. 42, 111; The Bridgeman Art Library: pp. 57 (© British Library, London/© British Library Board; all rights reserved), 58 (© Museum of Islamic Art, Cairo); courtesy of the Chile Pepper Institute at New Mexico State University, Las Cruces, NM: p. 139; courtesy of the City of Salem, Massachusetts: p. 118; Library of Congress, Washington, DC: p. 77; photos courtesy of McCormick & Company: pp. 129, 132; photo Françoise de Mulder/Roger Viollet/Rex Features: p. 99; Museu Nacional de Arte Antiga, Lisbon: pp. 66-67, 70; Patrimonio Nacional, Madrid: p. 72; Rijksmuseum, Amsterdam: p. 82; photos Roger-Viollet/Rex Features: pp. 95, 105, 127, 135, 137; Royal Botanic Garden, Edinburgh: pp. 11, 36, 84, 101; maps by Nancy Selden: pp. 24, 29, 40; Wellcome Images: pp. 13, 123; The Wellcome Trust: pp. 50, 54, 73.

Index